Advance Praise for *Appreciative Leadership*

"*Appreciative Leadership* makes clear connections between interpersonal style, organizational results, and the public good. It shows how to exercise principled leadership from any role in any organization."
—Barton Alexander
Vice President, Molson Coors Brewing Company

"*Appreciative Leadership* is both a philosophy and a methodology for positive engagement and change. It introduces us to the power within ourselves and others to see and do the right thing by our families, our communities, and the world."
—Gary M. Nelson, Ph.D.
Founding Member, Institute for Sustainable Development

"*Appreciative Leadership* is wholly consistent with the new science of positive emotions. Learning to cultivate positivity in ourselves and others unlocks a powerful new approach to leadership that will transform lives and organizations from the inside out."
—Barbara L. Fredrickson, Ph.D.
Author, *Positivity*; Professor, University of North Carolina

"If ever human communities needed Appreciative Leadership, now is the time. This book vividly illustrates how the world we want begins with our own commitment to get the best out of ourselves and others."
—Peter F. Norlin, Ph.D.
Executive Director, Organization Development Network

"This book is a must-read for leaders and aspiring leaders who want to transform their organizations by investing in what works. Its Five Core Strategies and user-friendly tips bring Appreciative Inquiry to life in a new and vital context."
—Dorrie K. Fontaine, Ph.D., RN, FAAN
Dean and Professor, School of Nursing, University of Virginia

"*Appreciative Leadership* is a must-read for leaders at all stages of their careers. Full of sound principles and skill-building practices, it prepares budding new leaders for the challenges of the modern world."
—William J. Hybl
Chairman and CEO, El Pomar Foundation

"Appreciative Leadership has become a way of life for me—and for many in my congregation who have embraced it. This book can help you do the same."

—Brigid Lawlor, RGS, JD
Congregational Leader, Sisters of the Good Shepherd

"This is a comprehensive guide on how to implement Appreciative Leadership. The authors' wisdom and research, blended with proven practices from many arenas, has produced a practical, wise book that you will reference for years to come."

—James C. and Dana G. Robinson
Coauthors, *Performance Consulting* and *Strategic Business Partner*

"*Appreciative Leadership* provides the key to unlock the hidden capacities of the many accomplished and brilliant people working in today's institutions."

—Paul R. G. Cunningham, MD, FACS
Dean, Brody School of Medicine, East Carolina University

"This insightful book charts a map for leadership strategies and practices in our post-industrial age. It tells us how to free our organizations from fear and encourage peak performance and positive change."

—William H. Hudnut III
Former Mayor, Indianapolis

"Learn how to discover the wisdom inherent in organizations and bring about positive results with this practical book."

—Dixie van de Flier Davis, Ed.D.
President and Executive Director, The Adoption Exchange

"*Appreciative Leadership* captures, nurtures, and expands on the power of Appreciative Inquiry. It shows us how to renew our organizations' cultures, inspiring universally high levels of contribution, engagement, and performance."

—Rick Pellett
President, Hunter Douglas Window Fashions Division

APPRECIATIVE LEADERSHIP

Focus on What Works to Drive Winning Performance
and Build a Thriving Organization

Diana Whitney, Ph.D.
Amanda Trosten–Bloom
Kae Rader

New York   Chicago   San Francisco   Lisbon   London
Madrid   Mexico City   Milan   New Delhi   San Juan
Seoul   Singapore   Sydney   Toronto

1 2 3 4 5 6 7 8 9 10   DOC / DOC   1 5 4 3 2 1 0

ISBN   978-0-07-171406-8
MHID   0-07-171406-5

Library of Congress Cataloging-Publication Data

Whitney, Diana Kaplin.
    Appreciative leadership : focus on what works to drive winning performance and build a thriving organization / Diana Whitney, Amanda Trosten-Bloom, and Kae Rader.
        p. cm.
    Includes bibliographical references.
    ISBN-13: 978-0-07-171406-8 (alk. paper)
    ISBN-10: 0-07-171406-5 (alk. paper)
1. Leadership. 2. Organizational effectiveness. 3. Organizational behavior.
I. Trosten-Bloom, Amanda, 1957- II. Rader, Kae. III. Title.
    HD57.7.W48 2010
    658.4'092—dc22   2009054141

LENA ECUNK'UNPI, HECEL OYATE KI NINPE KTE.

WE DO THESE THINGS SO THE PEOPLE MAY LIVE.

Contents

Foreword

KENNETH J. GERGEN

It has been a great privilege to count Diana Whitney, the senior author of this splendid work, as friend and colleague for over 25 years. From our very first meeting, a common interest in human communication was focal. For me, these interests took a scholarly turn; for Diana, they led to a sparkling career in organizational development.

My scholarly journey ultimately led me to explore the ways in which human communication gave rise to shared views of reality, morality, and rationality. Ultimately, it could be ventured, all that we hold to be worthwhile in life issues from communicative practices. Such views, often identified as social constructionist, were unsettling to many. They flew in the face of the scientific beliefs in objective truth, the philosophical beliefs in the foundations of logic, and the religious and humanistic beliefs in the existence of universal moral principles.

Yet, in discussions with Diana Whitney, the potentials for such ideas for practices of organizational change were breathtaking. Theories of the organization had long been based on a vision of the organization as a form of machine that would be subject to rational design and control. Organizational change was often based on top-down interventions, fortified by research on structure and function. And it was often unsuccessful.

From a social constructionist standpoint, the structuralist view was replaced with a vision of the organization as a living process in which every conversation in every location could affect—for good or ill—the future of the organization.

It was largely out of our excitement in such ideas and their practical implications that we joined with five other scholars and practitioners to form the Taos Institute, a nonprofit organization linking social constructionist ideas with societal practices for purposes of social change.

At the present juncture the Taos Institute—with some 200 associates from 18 nations—offers conferences and workshops, a Ph.D. program, online resources, low-cost publications, and more. However, at its inception, and owing to Suresh Srivastva and David Cooperrider's robust presence on the Institute's board of directors, our initial love affair was with the practice of Appreciative Inquiry. Here was a practice that optimally combined elements of constructionist theory with creative practices of collaboration.

The growth and application of Appreciative Inquiry over the past two decades has been nothing short of phenomenal. It is arguably the most powerful process of positive organizational change ever devised. Thousands of people from around the world have now used forms of Appreciative Inquiry to bring about change in organizations of all kinds—from entire nations and mammoth organizations to communities, families, and personal lives. Myriad articles and books attest to its inspiring power.

As one scans this impressive terrain, one is also struck with what might variously be viewed as its populist, democratic, or grassroots emphasis. That is, the appreciative movement honors the voices of all; its power rests on its synchronizing shared values and visions. Raise all the voices, it proposes, for in their resonance we move toward a positive destiny.

At the same time, the appreciative movement runs headlong into a centuries-old tradition of organizational management. This is a tradition celebrating individual leadership. From early accounts of charismatic leadership to more recent elaborations of effective management, the emphasis is on the qualities, traits, and skills of the individual in shaping the organization and mobilizing it in desired directions. This long-standing vision of the potentially powerful individual is now articulated in hundreds of popular books and training programs. Only a handful of volumes explore the possibility of modes of leadership in which collaboration takes precedence over individual prowess. And it is indeed difficult to locate works on leadership that draw their energies from the appreciative movement.

In effect, the present volume stands as a landmark in the theory and practice of organizational development. Whitney, and her talented colleagues—Amanda Trosten-Bloom and Kae Rader—expand the boundaries of understanding and practice. For them, leadership embedded in appreciative philosophy and practices is the key to thriving and successful organizational performance. Drawing from extensive consulting experiences with Appreciative Inquiry, along with close and collaborative research with leaders from wide-ranging organizations, the authors share a rich and compelling account of how an appreciative approach may function.

Drawing from the appreciative tradition, the authors offer five major orientations to harnessing the powers of appreciation. There is first the wisdom of inquiry, in which those in positions of leadership are invited to craft questions that can turn debilitating problems into opportunities for positive change. By drawing organizational members into mutual inquiry, bridges are built across functional domains, and ultimately an organizational culture can emerge in which all participants are valued. Then, through appreciative practices, participants are more inspired and engaged in the life of the organization. Third, there is the importance of bringing people together to cocreate the future of the organization. In the way such relations are organized, participants are energized to think and plan creatively. And finally, through these processes the individual-centered (or me-first) culture, so common in today's world, is replaced by decisions that celebrate the good of the whole.

This is rich fare indeed, and should stoke the fires of creative change in organizations great and small. However, in the longer run I think there is a deeper wisdom in this volume that may go unrecognized. It is the value—and indeed the profound promise—of understanding our world as relational process. We participate in a long tradition in which individual entities are focal. I am not speaking here only of individual persons, and the way we understand them in terms of their thoughts, values, desires, and so on. But we also focus our attention—both in science and daily life—on singular subject matters, such as the brain, the economy, medicine, housing, education, and so on. In effect, we carve our world into separated units or domains. Further, we treat these domains as static. That is, we presume that by continued study, we can accumulate knowledge of their nature and function. Such a presumption feeds from a view of the world in which the units remain the same over time.

Now consider the world from the standpoint embedded in the present account of Appreciative Leadership. As Whitney, Trosten-Bloom, and Rader propose, the success of the organization does not reside in the actions of individual actors but in the *relationships* among them. It is when these relationships thrive that participants are engaged, inspired, and committed. And if these relationships are mutually supportive, the potentials for creative change are maximal. In today's world, where global flows in ideas, values, people, and materials generate continuous challenges to routine and reason, an organization's potential for creative change is absolutely vital. And, should we extend the arts of appreciation to include all our relations—including peoples and environment—we may indeed move toward a viable and nurturing world.

Kenneth J. Gergen
President
Taos Institute

Acknowledgments

Diana

With loving gratitude to Brian and Shara: I am because you are. And with deep appreciation for the invisible forces that ignite my spirit and give meaning to my life.

Amanda

To my many teachers: Thank you for helping me find my voice and know my strength. To Barry, Hannah Joy, and Jessica: Your loving support makes everything possible.

Kae

To my parents, Esther and Harry Barr, for their unconditional love, which never ceases to bring out the best in me. And to my husband, Phil, my partner, my inspiration, my joy.

Together

We wish to acknowledge the contributions of Dr. James D. Ludema, our business partner and cocreator in the early stages of this book's development. Thank you, Jim, for your clear thinking and your generous spirit and for being a role model of Appreciative Leadership. And Dr. David L. Cooperrider whose innovative work provided the foundational principles of Appreciative Inquiry. Thank you, David, for all you do to make a positive difference in the world. And to our fantastic McGraw-Hill team, especially Fiona Sarne, Emily Carleton, Judith McCarthy, and Maureen Dennehy: Thank you for believing in us and in our ideas. It has been a joy working with you and the McGraw-Hill team.

Introduction

This book began over 50 years ago as we each stepped into leadership in our families, our Girl Scout troops, our classes, and our extracurricular activities at school. Early in our lives we were each called to leadership and wondered, what is good leadership? How do I do it or, better yet, *be* it?

Diana was asked to be the editor of her high school yearbook. She had no thought at the time of ever writing books. Her teachers saw her potential and offered her an opportunity to see it for herself. She is now an author or editor of 20 books—including her high school and college yearbooks and her Ph.D. dissertation! Along the same lines, Amanda's teachers and mentors invited her to speak publicly at school and in church, as even then her clear and hopeful messages moved people of all ages to action. Today she is an enthusiastic speaker and consultant who is able to inspire large groups of people toward positive change. For Kae, an early job in the Indianapolis mayor's office working with a team of talented and dedicated public service leaders was seminal. She gained lasting insights as they mindfully and consistently strove to make nonpartisan decisions for the benefit of the whole community. Now, as a seasoned consultant helping others work on behalf of their organizations, she still draws on those formative lessons. While our journeys have been different, they have brought us together, now, as colleagues and coauthors.

We are organization development consultants. We work with leadership teams to design and facilitate large-scale processes that result in whole-system positive change. We are accustomed to working with and supporting the creative collaboration of very large groups of people. Two hundred is a small group for us. Our clients include leadership teams from Hunter Douglas; the University of Virginia Health System; Sisters of the Good Shepherd; the cities of Longmont, Denver, and Boulder in Colorado; the U.S. Olympic Committee; British Airways; Verizon; Merck; Hewlett-Packard; and the United Religions Initiative—all very large organizations or communities.

Our work, called Appreciative Inquiry, is a high-engagement strengths-based process through which people collaboratively reinvent the vision, mission, strategy, culture, and identity of their organization or community. By participating in values-based inquiry and life-affirming dialogue, hundreds or thousands of people can collectively identify their positive core of strengths; envision a desired future; generate shared principles; and determine how they will go forward together. The process enhances both relationships and results—a winning combination.

Appreciative Inquiry has an impressive track record of success around the world and in a wide range of industries, sectors, and communities. Over the years we have wondered what makes it successful. Indeed, Diana and Amanda conducted a study and asked just that question. Their research is summarized in their best-selling book *The Power of Appreciative Inquiry.* Their findings point to Six Freedoms—unleashed through the Appreciative Inquiry process, that together forge a foundation for successful positive change. They are the freedoms to Be Known in Relationship, to Be Heard, to Dream in Community, to Choose to Contribute, to Act with Support, and to Be Positive. "When people realize that they can and do make a difference in relation to others," say the authors, "they experience true liberation. ... Appreciative Inquiry, through the Six Freedoms, creates a relational and narrative-rich context that becomes the path upon which the journey to liberation takes place."[1]

As is often the case, when one question is answered, another emerges. And so it was for us. With the Six Freedoms as our backdrop, we turned our attention to some related questions: What role does *leadership* play in liberating power, fostering positive change, and promoting ongoing organizational vitality and success? What is *unique, special,* and even *exciting* about this kind of leadership, at its best?

An Exploration of Leadership

In our quest to answer these questions and create a framework for talking about and teaching Appreciative Leadership, we moved through three phases: personal observations, appreciative interviews, and appreciative focus groups.

Personal Observations

We have worked with dozens of leadership teams to help them introduce Appreciative Inquiry to their organizations and communities and to use it for significant transformation. In the course of doing so, we began to notice that the leaders who chose Appreciative Inquiry as their vehicle for positive change had the following four things in common.

1. *They were willing to engage with other members of their organization or community to create a better way of doing business or living.* For example, Bishop William Swing, founder, and Charles Gibbs, executive director of the United Religions Initiative, both attended and fully participated in five annual international planning summits, a year-long series of design meetings, and multiple regional summits. At each meeting, they participated enthusiastically in conversations with people of different faiths, different countries, different ages, and different cultures. Similarly, leaders of Hunter Douglas Window Fashions Division, most particularly the president, Rick Pellett, engaged with the entire 1,000-person workforce, together with key customers, suppliers, and community members, in a process of forging a 10-year vision for the company. Finally, admirals in the U.S. Navy joined with other Navy personnel of all ranks and tenure during a series of highly inclusive, nonhierarchical gatherings focused on the development of "leadership at all levels."

2. *They were willing to learn and to change.* They did not simply expect it of others. For example, Rodrigo Loures, CEO of Nutrimental, SA, the Sisters of Good Shepherd, PMNA, and

an executive from Hunter Douglas all personally attended our Foundations of Appreciative Inquiry (AI) workshop before initiating changes in their organizations. All of these leaders continued to engage in learning and development opportunities with us, at Case Western Reserve University, and with other appreciative leaders, to build their capacities to work with AI. Perhaps more significantly, they were all open to learning from employees and stakeholders and to changing themselves as well as their organizations in the process.

Reflecting back on his leadership of Hunter Douglas Window Fashions Division's initiative, former vice president of human resources Mike Burns described the personal nature of his journey:

Leading this effort made a difference in virtually every aspect of my life. Day in and day out, it reminded me to look at positive possibilities rather than negative obstacles. It gave me tools to be a more compassionate, more inspiring parent, partner, and friend.

As I think about it, Appreciative Inquiry (AI) gave me tools that made my life better—for me, and for the people around me. What more could you ask?

Rick Pellett, president of the company, described similarly profound changes in himself and his worldview:

The AI work I did began to change me, almost right away. It got me asking questions—not just about the company, but about my life. It opened doors for me, and it invited me to consider where I was heading and whether it was the future I really wanted to live. It compelled me to take action to correct things that I'd simply chosen to live with for years and years and years.

I recognized that this experience might not create the same kind of "awakening" in everybody that it touched. But for me, it was revolutionary. And for many of the other hard-core, quick-deciding, bottom-line leaders that rise to the top in corporate America, it just might be life changing, for the better.

3. *These leaders truly believed in the power of the positive.* For executives like Theresa Bertram (then executive director of the Cathedral Foundation) and John Oechsle (former CIO for IHS), the positive was a direct line to high performance. When faced with low levels of employee morale and engagement, they both chose *positive* approaches to change. They understood that by studying what was successful and promising in their organizations, people would gain confidence and hope; but also that morale and performance would improve. Similarly, Margaret Browne, former manager of budget and finance for the city and county of Denver, Colorado, chose Appreciative Inquiry to address a $70 million budget shortfall, thereby achieving truly positive results. As these cases illustrate, belief in the power of the positive pays off in social as well as financial matters.

4. *These leaders cared about people, often describing the work of their organization or business in terms of helping people learn, grow, and develop.* Carolyn Miller, executive director of the Community Development Institute (CDI), is an exemplar of this kind of leadership. Leading from a stance of coach and mentor, she actively solicits people's hopes and dreams for their future, then supports them in taking on work that is consistent with those dreams. Her commitment to personal development is also reflected in the company's robust training budget, as well the regular, ongoing coaching that she and her fellow leaders engage in with their staffs.

As a result of our work with these exemplary leaders and others, we began to see that people and organizations could learn, grow, and change through a purposefully affirmative process. The old "no pain, no gain" view of personal development is not a requirement for people engaged in Appreciative Inquiry. When leaders participate with people in a positive and caring manner, people collectively transform their organizations and communities; and in the process they change.

Fueled by the insight that people change when they are surrounded by positive emotions and ideas, we designed and created our four-day intensive Appreciative Leadership Development Program (ALDP). It is the first leadership development program of its kind, and includes appreciative interviews, peer appreciative coaching, and 360-degree positive feedback. It is going strong today, with licensed trainers in four countries: Canada, Chile, Japan, and the United States.

Appreciative Interviews

As of this writing, approximately 100 interviews were conducted by participants in the Appreciative Leadership Development Program. Before attending the program, participants interviewed exemplary leaders—people they respect for who they are and how they lead. Then during the program they interviewed each other, discovering and sharing stories from their personal leadership journeys.

For more than five years, we compiled and reflected upon the ideas and stories garnered from these interviews. Indeed, many of them are woven throughout this book. Taken together, they led us to identify and distinguish the Five Core Strategies that are at the heart of Appreciative Leadership:

1. Inquiry
2. Illumination
3. Inclusion
4. Inspiration
5. Integrity

Here is a sampling of the meaningful quotes people shared with us from their interviews and experiences as leaders:

- "Always ask that next big question. Don't ask me to arrange the books on your shelf. Ask me which books to read."[2]

- "When we trust the people we lead, it calls them to be their best selves."[3]
- "Don't be like Betty. She was a negative role model. All I learned was what not to do."[4]
- "As you get to know a person, you realize they are a whole universe."[5]
- "If you don't know what to do, just keep talking to more people until it becomes clear."[6]

We found stories and quotes like these to be enlivening and generative, as they so clearly pointed to and reinforced our nascent ideas about the Five Core Strategies. Furthermore, as we listened to, looked into, and discussed them, one very provocative idea repeatedly emerged: great leadership—what we call *Appreciative Leadership*—is about positive power.

The idea of positive power got our attention, and so we began to speak and teach about it. In so doing, we discovered that it made sense and resonated deeply with people at all levels of leadership in organizations and communities. It seems that positive power is something everyone implicitly wants; yet few have an explicit framework for talking about it, doing it, or being it. Once again, we decided that research was in order: we needed to test the concepts of the Five Core Strategies of Appreciative Leadership and to explore what people mean when they talk about positive power.[7]

Appreciative Focus Groups

We hosted 10 focus groups on Appreciative Leadership and positive power. Our primary purpose was to more clearly understand what people want and need of leadership in order to be their best—to realize their potential. We wanted to hear, and learn about, exemplary leadership from people who have experienced it, in their own words and voices.

We asked participants questions about their high-point experiences of leadership, experiences of positive power, and the Five Core

Strategies of Appreciative Leadership. We also asked them each to offer up the one message that they would like leadership around the world to hear. Their ideas were simple and to the point. A dozen of the messages they shared are listed below; and others are sprinkled throughout the book:[7]

- Live what you espouse.
- Ask the questions nobody else does.
- Be engaged, be passionate, and be present.
- Consider all citizens your citizens.
- Take care of yourself, take care of others, and take care of this planet.
- Believe in the art of possibility.
- Learn to create harmony among differences.
- Be optimistic; have a can-do attitude.
- Give everyone a voice; collaborate.
- Take time to think, strategize, and check your plan.
- Love people; be people centric.
- Share vision and mission with everyone.

The focus group conversations were energizing and enlightening for everyone involved. Participants and facilitators alike came away with a clearer sense of what people want and expect of leadership, and how to be better leaders themselves. The Five Core Strategies were confirmed, and numerous specific practices were identified—many of which fill the pages that follow.

Introducing . . . Appreciative Leadership

The purpose of this book is to introduce you to the notions of Appreciative Leadership and positive power that have developed through our experiences and research. It is intended to give you a framework for understanding what Appreciative Leadership is, how to do it, and how to be it. These are not solely our ideas. They are ideas that have come together in this book, through us. Our dear friend Lakota sage and singer Howard Bad Hand, tells how musicians "catch" the songs they write. The songs show up in their hearts, minds, and ears, and they write them and sing them for the people. This is how it has been with this book. Together, we caught it. And we have written it for the people: those in leadership, those who aspire to leadership, and those who educate and cultivate future leadership. The ideas it contains have been shown to us, told to us, and given to us by colleagues and clients around the world. And now they are yours.

Overview of the Book

The book is written in short sections. You can start at the beginning and read it cover to cover; or you can scan the table of contents, find a section that interests you, and start there. Either way you are certain to find meaningful ideas and helpful practices.

 This is our pause button. When you come upon it in the book, we recommend that you take time for reflection. The activities and questions associated with this "pause" are meant to be provocative: to help you make meaning of, and remember, what you are reading. We also suggest that you make notes in the margins as you go, especially about your reflections and any insights that you may have. We wrote this book for you. Now it is time to make its ideas and practices your own.

The first chapter, "Appreciative Leadership Now," sets the stage. In it, we look at the context of leadership today, and offer our definition of Appreciative Leadership. We also assert the relational nature of Appreciative Leadership and describe how it creates ripples of positive results.

Chapter 2, "From Potential to Positive Power: The Five Core Strategies," briefly presents the findings of our research into Appreciative Leadership and positive power. We make the case, through stories and quotes, that people want leadership that is positively powerful. We draw distinctions between potential and power, and we offer a variety of ways through which human, organization, and community potential is relationally liberated and turned into positive power. Finally, we introduce the Five Core Strategies of Appreciative Leadership: inquiry, illumination, inclusion, inspiration, and integrity.

Chapters 3 through 7 present the Five Core Strategies in detail. A chapter is dedicated to each, complete with definitions, exemplary case examples, and specific Appreciative Leadership practices. Each of these five chapters ends with a summary of practices and a list of books and Web sites for further consideration.

In Chapter 3, "The Wisdom of Inquiry: Leading with Positively Powerful Questions," we make it clear that the questions leaders ask are very influential—for better or for worse. And we offer specific Appreciative Leadership practices for crafting and asking positively powerful questions.

Chapter 4, "The Art of Illumination: Bringing out the Best of People and Situations," establishes the strengths-based orientation of Appreciative Leadership. We ground it in the concept of Appreciative Intelligence—the capacity to see inherent positive potential—and we offer a wide range of practices for discovering strengths, identifying the root causes of success, and elevating performance.

In Chapter 5, "The Genius of Inclusion: Engaging with People to Cocreate the Future," we make the case for including all the people whose future it is in dialogue and decisions about the future. We take a stand that says Appreciative Leadership is about including people whose voices have not previously been in the conversation. We offer up practices to engage others—ranging from one other person to thousands.

Chapter 6, "The Courage of Inspiration: Awakening the Creative Spirit," shows you that creativity, inspiration, and hope are essential for high performance and positive change. We describe the elements of hope—vision, a path forward, and the confidence that resources are accessible—and we offer specific practices for each.

The last of the chapters on the Five Core Strategies is Chapter 7, "The Path of Integrity: Making Choices for the Good of the Whole." In it we liken integrity to wholeness. On a personal level, this means being true to yourself. On an organizational level, it means working in service to the whole. On a global level, it is a call for leaders to balance the triple bottom line—people, profit, and planet.

In Chapter 8, "Making a Positive Difference with Appreciative Leadership," we reinforce our belief that each individual has a unique "domain of positive power." We continue by describing five specific ways readers will make a positive difference in the world as they move more deeply into the practice of Appreciative Leadership to "*be the change* they wish to see in the world." [8]

In the Conclusion, we summarize the book's key messages, and we provide a closing activity that will enable readers to synthesize what they have learned by writing their leadership story. Finally, we share our vision for the future of Appreciative Leadership.

Now—begin your exploration! This is your book. It is filled with ideas about Appreciative Leadership and positive power. Some of what you read will be new to you, and some will seem familiar. We hope that, as you read and reflect upon the new, it will expand who you are as a leader and that, as you read and reflect upon the familiar, it will affirm you and lift your self-confidence and courage as a leader. Above all, we hope that you will find the many practices described throughout this book relevant to your work, and that these practices will be easy for you to adopt and align with your deepest values and goals.

ONE

Appreciative Leadership Now

The world has changed. Approaches to leadership that served well in the past do not address the challenges of the twenty-first century. Appreciative Leadership does.

We have crossed a threshold to a new era: one that demands a radical shift in leadership strategies and practices. Few places on the planet are untouched by the "progress of the industrial age" and the "dawning of the electronic age." Cities and local markets from New York to Chang Mai to Santiago to Lahore all feature cars, computers, and cell phones. Our planet is wrapped in a web of airplane routes, satellite orbits, and telecommunication signals.

New Approaches to Leadership for the New Global Society

This transformation from an industrial age to an electronic age brings us face to face with the reality of our interdependence. As inhabitants of the earth, we are connected—from the air we breathe, to the water we drink, to the energy that powers our lifestyles, to the pain, hunger, and sorrow in the eyes of children around the world. With the help of technology, we have discovered, as if for the first time, something that has always been and will always be: *we are all related.*

Acknowledgment of this interdependence leads us to profoundly shift what we wish for and expect from leadership. Success in the future will go to those who help us come into harmony, among ourselves and with the planet—to those who help us to thrive as one global community. President of the World Business Academy Rinaldo Brutoco affirmed this when he stated, "Now more than ever, the world business community must face the inescapable conclusion, at the core of the Academy's very existence: business must be willing to become responsible for the whole of global society."[1]

To meet this challenge, leadership now—in the twenty-first century—must be aware of and respond to four trends currently defining the social milieu of organizations and communities:

1. *New generations have come of age.* Younger people expect different things from work, from community, and from leadership than the generations that preceded them. Today, people want to be engaged and heard. They want to be involved in the decisions that affect them and to be acknowledged for a job well done.

2. *Diversity is the norm.* Organizations and communities are no longer homogeneous. Whether local or global, small town or corporate, they are composed of people with a wide variety of ethnic and cultural backgrounds, of differing ages and preferences. Speaking many languages and sharing many different histories, people in today's organizations want leadership to be collaborative and just.

3. *Institutions are being reinvented.* The context of leadership is no longer stable or predictable. In all sectors of industry and society, institutions have failed and are being reimagined and redesigned. These new institutions are more fluid and more agile. In them, distributed leadership and power emerges as people self-organize to meet the needs of the whole.

4. *Holistic, sustainable approaches are essential.* Today's decisions will cast the die for generations to come. The most pressing social, economic, environmental, and political challenges of our time are global in nature. They cannot be resolved by one person, one country, or one business. They require unprecedented appreciation of differences and collaboration. In short, they call for Appreciative Leadership.

What Is Appreciative Leadership?

Appreciative Leadership is a philosophy, a way of being and a set of strategies that give rise to practices applicable across industries, sectors, and arenas of collaborative action. The following definition of Appreciative Leadership is full of potential. As you read it ask yourself, "What does this mean to me and for the way I work?" We also suggest that you offer it up for discussion among colleagues and team members. Read it to them and discuss, "What does this mean for us and for the way we work together?"

> *Appreciative Leadership* is the relational capacity to mobilize creative potential and turn it into positive power—to set in motion positive ripples of confidence, energy, enthusiasm, and performance—to make a positive difference in the world.

Embedded in this definition are four formative ideas about Appreciative Leadership: (1) it is relational; (2) it is positive; (3) it is about turning potential into positive power; and (4) it has rippling effects. You may also realize, as many others have, that each of these four ideas represents a paradigm shift: a clear movement away from the habitual, traditional, and individualistic command and control practices of leadership toward "a new normal": the positive, socially generative principles, strategies, and practices of Appreciative Leadership.

Appreciative Leadership Is a Relational Capacity

All work, indeed all life, occurs in relationship. It is our experience that while there are individuals called "leaders" and there are individuals that others perceive as leaders, nothing of worth happens without the involvement of many people. Professor Kenneth Gergen offers the most substantive understanding of relational capacities in his book *Relational Being*.[2] In it he describes the paradigm shift from "individualistic" views of leadership to "relational" views, saying, "None of the qualities attributed to good leaders stands alone. Alone, one cannot be inspiring, visionary, humble, or flexible. These qualities are the achievements of a coactive process in which others' affirmation is essential. A charismatic leader is only charismatic by virtue of others who treat him or her in this way; remove the glitter in their eyes and the 'charisma' turns to dust. ... Leadership resides in the confluence."[3]

We have chosen, therefore, to write about leadership: the relational processes and practices through which people come together to make things happen. Sometimes people come together as leaders and followers. Sometimes they do this as equals, each bringing different strengths, resources, and capacities; other times they come together as diverse stakeholders collaborating to cocreate (or coauthor) something like a better business model, a more environmentally friendly product, or a more socially and economically feasible health care system. No matter what the form, relationships are at the heart of leadership and its capacity to make things happen. Imagine the confluence of relationships in this brief story:

> Patricia Arenas, former director of Havana's Human Change Project, has traveled around the world to culturally diverse countries, including Russia, Mexico, the United States, the United Kingdom, and Denmark, to study and to share her work. She has said, "It's the same on the ground here in Cuba as it is most places; it's all about the people and relationships."

Curious to explore the positive collaborative potential of the Appreciative Inquiry (AI) process in Cuba, she and her colleagues invited a team of Appreciative Inquiry experts led by Dr. Diana Whitney to Cuba for research. The question was, "How might Appreciative Inquiry support the work of the Human Change Project, throughout the country, with members of community and business organizations?"

Fifty Cuban organizational consultants met with the American researchers for two days. They explored both how and where to experiment with the AI process. Patricia commented at the time, "Building on what already works well seems hardly revolutionary, but it really is. It is a big change for people to stay focused on and study what's working. They are so used to talking about what needs to be fixed." Almost a year later, the research showed that Appreciative Inquiry was being used to revamp university curriculums, to manage the cleanup of the Bay of Havana, and to build on the many strengths of Cuba's world-famous public health system.

The idea of leadership as a relational capacity resonates with the South African notion of *ubuntu*. From the Zulu and Xhosa languages, the word *ubuntu* is translated to mean, "I am because you are—I can only be a person through others."[4] It suggests that a leader's identity, indeed anyone's identity, rests at the center of relatedness. Appreciative leaders "are" because of the people with whom they work and serve. Firefighters know this perhaps better than anyone else:

Coloradans still remember the devastating wildfires of 2002 triggered by a severe drought. Federal and state agencies struggled for months to douse the fierce blazes that swept through forests and towns. Volunteer fire departments made up of families, friends, and neighbors in the small mountain communities simply didn't have the fire protective clothing or equipment to adequately fight off a threat of this magnitude. Seeing this, a charitable foundation quickly sent representatives on site with checks in hand to offer support. Foundation representatives weren't prepared for the reaction they received. Rather than accepting the full amount, many fire chiefs accepted only a portion of the funding and asked that the remaining funds be given to neighboring fire departments also in need.

Relational capacity does not mean, as is so frequently taught, that you must therefore go out and "make relationships," as if they don't already exist, in order to work or to live well. Instead, it means that you must accept relationships as always present, as here from the beginning, as surrounding us, and as infusing us with their presence. Your Appreciative Leadership task is then to become relationally aware, to tune into patterns of relationship and collaboration—that is, to see, hear, sense, and affirm what is already happening in order to best relate to it and perform with it.

We experienced a deeply moving example of this a number of years ago, at a Taos Institute conference in Belgium. The "polyphonic" singing group Capella Pratensis performed Gregorian chants in a historic chapel. We were enchanted by the group's music and later by their description of their process: They arrive early to the space where they will perform. They listen to the sounds already present, and when they sing, they sing into and in relation to the sounds of the space. At that moment we could not imagine a more beautiful sound or a more relational process.

The relational capacity of Appreciative Leadership, to tune into positive relational patterns—what we call the *positive core* of any person or group—and to work with them, is a starting point for all positive change. It is especially relevant in organizations and communities when the configuration of relationships need to change—for example, when a new member joins a team, a department gets a new head, two units or organizations merge, or when a new project is launched. In all cases, Appreciative Leadership is implicitly and explicitly relational, living and working with awareness of and care for the group's impact upon other people, all living beings, and the earth.

Appreciative Leadership Is a Positive Worldview

In the closing chapter of their book *Appreciative Leaders: In the Eye of the Beholder,* consultants Marge Schiller, Bea Mah Holland, and Deanna Riley describe Appreciative Leadership as a "worldview."[5] Indeed, it is a worldview—that is, it is a set of beliefs and a way of seeing the world, people, and situations—that is uniquely and, by choice, positive and life affirming. And as such, this positive worldview informs all that is Appreciative Leadership: its identity, strategies, practices, and results.

Appreciative leaders hold each and every person in positive regard. They look through appreciative eyes to see the best of people. They seek to treat all individuals positively, with respect and dignity, no matter their age, gender, race, religion, or culture—even education or experience. They believe that everyone has positive potential—a positive core of strengths and a passionate calling to be fulfilled—and they seek to bring that forward and nurture it. Take Mary Beth's story as an example. Having contributed positively to her organization for nearly 10 years as the manager of human resources, she approached her boss asking to move into the operations side of the business. Together, she and her boss negotiated a plan: she would attend a few outside classes and workshops to obtain some crucial skills she was missing, and the boss would find a new place for her in the organization, where she could learn and grow with support. Within a year, the transfer was achieved. Nearly a decade later, she serves as a senior operations leader in one of the company's largest and most profitable business units.[6]

Appreciative leaders see the glass as half full. They look for and are able to consistently see the inherent positive potential in any situation, no matter how dire it may seem. They understand the value of positive images to inspire and give hope. They share stories of success and offer images of possibility so that others have a positive path forward. Rather than talking about what cannot happen, what the problem is, or why things won't work, they talk about what is needed, what is possible, and what will be done. Their positive worldview often takes form as a can-do attitude.

On the heels of a narrow loss in the New Hampshire primary election of 2008, soon-to-be-president Barack Obama demonstrated this positive worldview in what was described by some as one of the most inspiring concession speeches ever delivered:

> For most of this campaign, we were far behind. We always knew our climb would be steep. But in record numbers, you came out, and you spoke up for change. And with your voices and your votes, you made it clear that at this moment, in this election, there is something happening in America. … We are ready to take this country in a fundamentally new direction.
>
> We know the battle ahead will be long. But always remember that, no matter what obstacles stand in our way, nothing can stand in the way of the power of millions of voices calling for change. …
>
> We've been asked to pause for a reality check. We've been warned against offering the people of this nation false hope. But in the unlikely story that is America, there has never been anything false about hope. For when we have faced down impossible odds, when we've been told we're not ready or that we shouldn't try or that we can't, generations of Americans have responded with a simple creed that sums up the spirit of a people: Yes, we can. Yes, we can. Yes, we can.[7]

Appreciative leaders are affirmative by choice. They use positive approaches to get positive results. A central measure of success is, "Contribute good to the day." What this means is that at the end of the day, appreciative leaders can describe what they did that day to add value to others, to bring out the best of people or situations, and/or to set positive ripples in motion.

Appreciative Leadership Turns Potential into Positive Power

Appreciative Leadership is more than a worldview. It is a way of being—a set of strategies and related practices—that makes things happen and gets results. Appreciative Leadership assumes that each person has a positive core, an implicit source of goodness and positive potential awaiting discovery, recognition, and realization. Appreciative Leadership senses potential and turns it into positive power—that is, into life-affirming results. Trusting that with few exceptions, each person has the capacity to make a meaningful contribution, appreciative leaders see it as their job to draw out and nurture potential and to ensure conditions for its success. In so doing, they turn human potential into positive power.

Appreciative leaders often see potential in people and situations where others do not. When they do see potential, they talk about it, engage with others, and act on it. As the following story shows, appreciative leaders see potential and bring forth positive power even in situations of great distress:

After living and working in the United States for 20 years as a successful beautician, Zemi Yenus returned to her home of Addis Ababa, Ethiopia, to be with family. She quickly became troubled by the numbers of child prostitutes she saw on the streets and began to imagine what their lives would be like if their outer beauty was used differently. Little by little and child by child she transformed her home-based beauty parlor into a beauty school that has graduated over 150 skilled beauticians.

Besides learning technical beautician skills, the students learn how to organize and run a small business, how to work as a team, and how to use their own transformations to give back to the community. Classes are, to a large degree, planned and organized by the former street kids. Boys and girls learn together to break stereotypes and gender roles. Rap sessions are held once a week, giving students and alumni an opportunity to celebrate learning and help each other overcome challenges like abuse at home or temptations to make more money on the streets. Most rap sessions also include some form of a talent show to highlight students' unique strengths and creativity.

Costs associated with the education program are heavily subsidized by local and international grants, but the longer-term plan is that the network of beauty parlors will some day be able to fund the education/transformation of other students and provide graduates with a strong employment path. After visiting the school recently, an international aid worker commented, "It was incredible to see the self-confidence of a 15-year-old girl running a meeting of 50 students. She facilitated in such a way that the boy running the meeting next week would know where she left off and where he would begin. I thought to myself, 'Wow, if we could all work that way, what a world we would have.'"

In addition to starting the NIA Foundation to help Ethiopia's street kids, Zemi has also built on her experience to start Ethiopia's only center for autistic children.

With the support of Appreciative Leadership, many people outgrow the limits of their realities and move into a larger more appreciative world—like lotus flowers growing from the mud. Professor David Cooperrider has suggested that this happens through inquiry.

He has written, "The appreciative leader enlarges everyone's knowledge and vision of the appreciable world—all the strengths, capacities, and potentials—not by having solid answers but with expansive questions. It is precisely through inquiry itself that appreciative leaders realize and unleash not their own but other people's genius."[8] Indeed, by engaging with people in communication, inquiry, and collaboration, you can unleash potential, generate performance, and ensure the creation of worthy results.

Appreciative Leadership Sets Positive Ripples in Motion

Through their words, actions, and relationships, appreciative leaders start waves of positive change rippling outward, often to destinations unknown. You know how this goes: someone at work stops you and tells you that you did a great job, that he or she would have missed his or her delivery date without your contribution. It lifts your spirit. When you go home, you tell your son, thanks for recycling the trash, something you don't often say to him because it's his job and he's just supposed to do it. He nods at your approval. The next day after lunch at school, he offers to put his friend's empty soda can in the recycle bin. His friend also says thanks. Your son is on his way to a habit of environmental consciousness that will last a lifetime. Positive ripples keep magnifying and multiplying through relationships in meaningful, and often surprising, ways and directions.

One of the most extraordinary positive ripples of our time got started by Professor David Cooperrider and his colleagues at Case Western Reserve University. When their team gave birth to Appreciative Inquiry in the mid–1980s, they had no idea that it would ripple out and wrap the world in positive possibilities. A few of the notable ripples have included the following:

- *From the university to the world:* In 1990 USAID funded the Global Excellence in Management Program (GEM) at Case Western Reserve University to promote organizational excellence and capacity building among development organizations working worldwide. Appreciative Inquiry served as the foundational theory and practice.

- *Award-winning corporate culture change:* Appreciative Inquiry was used successfully by companies such as Hunter Douglas Window Fashions Division, Nutrimental SA, and Roadway Express. GTE corporation (now Verizon) received the American Society for Training & Development (ASTD) "Best Organization Change Award" for the vanguard work done over two years guided by Dr. David Cooperrider and Dr. Diana Whitney.

- *Community development:* Imagine Chicago launched Appreciative Inquiry as a viable process for community development. Projects modeled on the Imagine Chicago projects have been conducted elsewhere in cities, states, and countries with great success—for example, Imagine Dallas, Imagine West Australia, and Imagine Chile.

- *International education:* Practitioner workshops and university degree programs are offered on the Appreciative Inquiry process. Case Western Reserve University continues to be a center for research and graduate education. Three international Appreciative Inquiry conferences have been held, the most recent in Nepal in 2009.

- *Publications:* Hundreds of books including the best-selling *Power of Appreciative Inquiry,* the *AI Practitioner Journal,* and numerous academic articles have been written and translated into dozens of languages, thereby extending the international reach of Appreciative Inquiry.

One last ripple of note: Our work with Appreciative Inquiry brought us together as colleagues. It introduced us to many of the people and organizations whose stories fill these pages. And it provided the seminal worldview upon which Appreciative Leadership is founded. For all of this we are grateful.

TWO

From Potential to Positive Power: The Five Core Strategies

THE TURNAROUND

The team had great potential; it just wasn't working well at the time. All of the six directors were young and energetic, extremely intelligent and creative. Each had track records of success in previous positions. But they had been "silenced" by a succession of authoritarian leaders rotated through the division in previous years. Consequently, they greeted Don, the new vice president with a mixture of caution and skepticism.

It didn't take long for things to start changing. Don constantly wandered around, asking questions about how things worked, what the team was trying to accomplish, and why. He was sincerely interested. He publicly acknowledged people's contributions, and encouraged members of the team to go to one another for help. Weekly leadership team meetings became the norm. The meetings included corporate and functional updates, as well as open dialogue about new directions and challenges. Don's warm and inclusive style enabled him to connect with even the most cautious in the group.

As weeks passed, however, people began complaining about one another's work. They began competing for his attention, asking Don to take sides in complex or contentious decisions. He did as he was asked at first; then he expressed concern. One day, having been called in to moderate a particularly petty dispute, he tried a new approach: "You two need to work this out. You're smart, you have great experience, and together you know what needs to be done. I'm leaving the room. Now you work it out." The two directors sat stone silent in the wake of his departure. First one apologized, then the other asked a question—then they got to work, together.

Within six months, the team was transformed. Their trust in one another was infectious—their mutual support palpable. The units that they collectively managed thrived, as together they ignited enthusiasm and creativity at all levels. People from other divisions clambered to transfer in. Profits soared. On their one-year anniversary, the president recognized the team for its outstanding contribution to the company. Each member of the team eventually went on to lead another organization—but all of them continued to stay in touch—sometimes asking for help, sometimes simply catching up, and sometimes recalling how much they had learned from Don.

Appreciative Leadership mobilizes creative potential and transforms it into positive power. This happens through reflection, inquiry, and dialogue among people. Potential rests unfulfilled until it is manifested through human discourse—given form in language, words, and ultimately actions. Human potential, situational potential, organizational potential, and community potential—strengths, capacities, abilities, and talents—remain implicit until "spoken into life."

Words, language, and metaphors are among the most versatile tools of Appreciative Leadership. They evoke meaning, emotions, and resonance among people. As such, they can either reinforce habitual ways of being, or they can generate transformation. Habits are held in place and the status quo is maintained through words and language. Consider the leadership habits evoked by words such as *boss, superior, employees, subordinates,* and *bureaucracy*. In contrast, what leadership habits are prompted when you hear words such as *coach, mentor, associate, business partner, relational responsibility,* and *self-organizing system*? Each set of words contains a world of relationships, meanings, and accepted performances. Just as words are expressed, so is the world they contain.

Words and language are also the tools of transformation—sometimes welcome, and sometimes not! Remember the first time you heard the word *Google* or *blog* or *Wikipedia*? How and with whom did you make meaning of these strange vocabularies when you first heard them? Who and what led them to become meaningful resources for you? What has been your process for turning their latent potential into power to help you get results and make a positive difference? How has your relationship with technology changed in the process? How has the story you tell about yourself and technology changed? As your answers to these questions most likely suggest: novelty is an invitation to talk with others, to explore potential, and make meaning of it. In the process, change happens.

Appreciative Leadership chooses and uses words, metaphors, and language to create the worlds they most desire: to stimulate potential, to name it, to make meaning of it, and to bring it to life through inquiry and dialogue with others.

It's Okay to Be Powerful

Merriam-Webster's definition of *power*—"the ability or capacity to act or perform effectively"[1]—indirectly suggests that it is okay to be powerful. When would you not want this? When would you not want to act or perform effectively? In order to be effective, you must be powerful—in your own way. Being and feeling powerful are essential to optimal performance.

In his 1994 inaugural address, one of the noblest leaders of our time, Nelson Mandela, suggested that people fear their own power more than their weakness:

> Our deepest fear is not that we are inadequate. Our deepest fear is that we are powerful beyond measure. It is our Light, not our Darkness, that frightens us. We ask ourselves, who am I to be brilliant, gorgeous, talented, fabulous? Actually, who are you not to be? You are a child of God. Your playing small does not serve the World. There is nothing enlightened about shrinking so that other people won't feel insecure around you. We were born to manifest the glory of God that is within us. It is not just in some of us; it is in everyone. As we let our own light shine, we unconsciously give other people permission to do the same. As we are liberated from our fear, our presence automatically liberates others.[2]

So why do people fear being powerful? Why do they not give their best? Maybe they simply don't know that *it is okay to be powerful.* Perhaps they don't see other people around them being powerful; or they see others being punished for voicing their opinions or otherwise taking risks. Perhaps they have never learned how to express themselves freely and honestly; or they have been criticized for doing so at work or at home. Perhaps they have not learned what their own strengths are or how to recognize other people's strengths. In essence, they do not feel safe or supported to be powerful. They don't know that they will be okay being powerful.

A turning point came in a union and management retreat we were facilitating when one of the union executives said this about the company workforce:

We are at 40 to 50 percent capacity right now. Our people are not giving their best. They feel beaten down, and they are acting like turtles—pulling into their shells for protection. I know we cannot afford to hire more people. The only option we have is to create a management style that draws people out, makes them feel safe, and creates the kind of workplace where they can be open with their thoughts and ideas.

On the last day of the retreat, the combined union and management team committed to seven collaborative aspirations, the first of which was to become an empowered work culture.

Positively powerful leadership is a two-sided coin. On one side, it is about being powerful: bringing your best forward, giving voice to what matters to you, and engaging with others in creating a world that works for all. And on the other, it is about helping others to be powerful: knowing their strengths, having confidence and opportunities to share their ideas, and seeking out support, learning, and collaboration to contribute their best.

 Pause and reflect for a moment. Are people in your organization pulled inside their shells like turtles playing it safe, or are they expressing themselves in positively powerful ways? How about you: Are you at the top of your game? What is it about your work environment that enables you to be and feel powerful? How are you sharing the power?

People Want Positively Powerful Leadership

Appreciative Leadership embraces collaborative practices and shared leadership, as well as what is traditionally considered the leader-follower relationship. While we do believe that everyone has leadership potential, our experience has shown that not everyone wants to be a leader or part of a leadership team. Some people are quite content and can be highly productive taking the lead from others. And some people are clearly at their best when they are in support of others who do the leading. It is from this vantage point that we conducted our research. We sought to understand what people want from leadership: what they consider exemplary leadership, and how it transforms potential to generate elevated performance, personally and collectively.

In the focus groups we conducted, people got excited about the idea of positive power. They liked hearing the words *positive* and *power* put together. They readily recalled experiences of positive power and talked freely about what it meant to them. As you can see from the following comments, their ideas about positive power included both how things are done and the nature of results achieved. They described positive power in these ways:

- Drawing on what is positive about the situation. Making the best of the situation you are in.
- Having a good upbeat attitude to get the job done.
- Using positive reinforcement and positive words, as well as vocalizing ideas that have shown positive results in the past.
- Being a force for the greater good; using authority for good and not evil.
- Being able to create positive change.
- Finding the positive in others—taking time to understand them and find out what they need to be part of a functioning team.
- A magnetic pull that draws you to be part of it.
- The ability to achieve positive end results.
- Letting people make decisions about their own lives.
- I like to follow them because I like them and they have gained my respect, not because they are the boss.

People wanted positive power in all aspects of their work life: they wanted to feel it; they wanted to participate in it; and they wanted the results it can create. Taken together, the people interviewed portrayed positive power on four levels: personal, one-to-one, team, and whole organization. Many of those who described it as *a personal capacity* also said that it was within their own control and that it had to do with how they think about and talk about their work. Their comments suggest that one way to get positive results is to choose to focus on positive possibilities:

- I think positive power is personal and within my own control.
- It's how I think about things. I decided to opt out of the recession. I've had a great year as a real estate broker. I simply don't have time for all this adversity. This is what positive power means to me.
- It's your energy, what you radiate. It's when the energy that surrounds you and your actions is clear. There is no confusion or tension with positive power.

Others who were interviewed said that they recognized and valued positive power as an *interpersonal capacity* that generates respect and engagement. They suggested that people are motivated by and want to be around people who are positive. They described a mutually respectful responsiveness that comes with positive power, a positive contagion that spreads when nurtured:

- It's exhilarating to meet someone with positive power. If he or she is excited about something, I tend to get more engaged. It is a kind of happiness.
- It's a person I respect and someone who respects me. It's someone who uses influence positively, and I can go to that person for help and he or she won't think less of me. Anyone who wants pearls of wisdom, advice, or counsel would go to this person.
- Truly powerful leaders make sure that everyone around them is successful in what they do. Other people's success is their success.

Many of the people we interviewed shared stories of how positive power emerged in groups and teams. They described positive power and performance as a *collective capacity*—the result of collaboration and mutual support:

- Positive power is working with other organizations leveraging resources to generate positive outcomes. It represents partnerships and collaborations. If the right people are at the table, they can make decisions and move things forward for the greater good. All can be stronger. This is especially important right now for nonprofits.

- The result of positivity is that it brings up the whole group and we can sell more. We can actually measure it in sales performance. I am sure it must work for other functions too.

- I like to host "advances" rather than "retreats." When I took over as manager, I took my whole department to the top of Pikes Peak for an advance, to get a new view. We didn't plan our work; we planned how we would support each other as a team. It's been five years now, and we are the most supportive and high performing team I have ever worked with. We are powerful.

And finally, positive power was depicted as *a characteristic of the whole organization*. Participants suggested that a work environment, the way business is done, and even the culture of an organization can all be models of positive power. They also noted that it takes work to keep up the positive because there is a societal bias toward negativity:

- We treat positivity as our normal way of doing business. It is important to our success. If an employee gets chewed out and is in a negative mindset, he or she will miss the next sale when a new client walks in the door. Being negative is a hole we all have to keep digging ourselves out of. We all have to keep on top and rolling in the spirit of positive power.

- We have a culture of positive power. It had to be developed and maintained, and it had to be required and expected of everyone in the organization. We had to overcome the societal negativity that is out there. As leaders, we constantly give employees affirmation about what they are doing right and how they are doing it. Even if it is small, we build incrementally on the things that people are doing right. Soon it becomes the experience they have of work.

- It has a lot to do with the flow of communication. If you don't pump positivity into the system, negativity will set in on its own. When there is an absence of information, people begin to fear the unknown. ... Positivity has to be trained at work because outside of work, in society, in the media, things are mostly negative.

One final and important note from our interviews: Positive power was portrayed as an antidote to criticism and a source of risk taking. People and groups with positive power, who are grounded in their own thinking and ideas, were described as less afraid of criticism, more open to hearing and learning what other people think and feel, and more likely to take risks.

The message is clear: it takes positively powerful leadership to discover and nurture the positive power and elevated performance of other people.

Surprising Sources of Creative Potential

Creative potential is sometimes quite apparent. It's what you look for when you are skimming résumés, interviewing job candidates, and selecting team members. It's what you hear when you ask people to share success stories and depict best practices. It's what you demonstrate when you speak from your heart, give voice to your innovative intentions, or express your commitment to positive change.

More often, however, creative potential rests quietly awaiting discovery. We are often surprised when we invite people to discover their strengths and then use their discoveries to help them create images of their ideal future. Among the ranks of engineers, managers, physicians, executives, and social workers, for example, we have found undiscovered visionaries, long-range planners, cheerleaders, artists, musicians, and poets—all waiting to be seen and to be called upon to give their best. A workshop participant summed it up this way:

Appreciative Leadership is like mining. You know the gems are there, you just don't know where they are. You have to dig for them. This changes everything I thought about people. I used to live by the saying "What you see is what you get." Well, now I understand that I have to listen better, ask more questions, and dig for the gems that are not so readily apparent. I need to look and listen with more confidence in people.

We call this *seeing with "appreciative eyes."* As you practice seeing with your appreciative eyes, you too will be surprised by the infinite relational potential you will discover. Table 2-1 offers eight "mining sites"—places you might begin your quest for as yet unexpressed positive potential.

TABLE 2-1 EIGHT SURPRISING SOURCES OF POSITIVE POTENTIAL	
1. Strengths	*Success breeds success.* Study strengths, capabilities and high performance patterns.
2. Past Success	*History is a source of positive possibility.* Share stories of success from the past.
3. Cynicism	*Behind every cynical statement there is a dream wanting to be realized.* Ask about the dream; listen for it and reflect it.
4. Big Emotions	*Validation releases emotions and creates a clearing for ideas.* Listen with compassion; affirm and reflect feelings.
5. Edgy Ideas	*Innovation lives on the edge. It is never the norm.* Seek out and playfully consider unlikely and disliked ideas.
6. Connectivity	*New connections create new opportunities.* Reach out and get to know new people, and people anew.
7. Opposition	*Unity is harmony among differences.* Seek out people with whom you disagree. Respectfully seek a new "mash" of ideas that resonates with all.
8. Novelty	*Novelty is the seed of learning.* Regularly try new things, try new ways of doing things, and reflect upon ideas that are new to you.

Each of the eight sources of positive potential requires you to look, listen, and interact with others appreciatively, with curiosity and compassion. Many of the sources invite courage on your part: to engage with people who are different from you, to consider unfavorable ideas, and to allow yourself be influenced and changed in the process.

The liberation of creative potential is a generative journey. It is an opening to innovation, and to the mysterious uncertainty of human organizing. It is an invitation to collaborative creativity, to learn as you go and cocreate along the way. It is the way of Appreciative Leadership, enacted through the Five Core Strategies and a myriad of positive practices.

Five Core Strategies of Appreciative Leadership

Our research on Appreciative Leadership and positive power, our experience as executive coaches, and the success of our work and that of our colleagues facilitating large-scale transformation using Appreciative Inquiry all coalesce into five areas of relational practice—what we call the *Five Core Strategies of Appreciative Leadership*. They are presented in Table 2-2. Each strategy is a means by which Appreciative Leadership successfully unleashes potential and elevates positive performance.

Each of the Five Core Strategies meets a different need that people have for high performance: to know they belong; to feel valued for what

TABLE 2-2 FIVE CORE STRATEGIES OF APPRECIATIVE LEADERSHIP	
Inquiry	Ask positively powerful questions.
Illumination	Bring out the best of people and situations.
Inclusion	Engage with people to coauthor the future.
Inspiration	Awaken the creative spirit.
Integrity	Make choices for the good of the whole.

they have to contribute; to know where the organization or community is headed; to know that excellence is expected and can be depended on; and to know that they are contributing to the greater good.

- *Inquiry lets people know that you value them and their contributions.* When you ask people to share their thoughts and feelings—their stories of success or ideas for the future—and you sincerely listen to what they have to say, you are telling them, "I value you and your thinking."

- *Illumination helps people understand how they can best contribute.* Through the practices of illumination you can help people learn about their strengths and the strengths of others. You give them confidence and encouragement to express themselves, take risks, and support others in working from their strengths.

- *Inclusion gives people a sense of belonging.* When you practice inclusion, you open the door for collaboration and cocreation. This, in turn, creates an environment in which people feel they are a part of something. When they feel part of something, they care for it.

- *Inspiration provides people with a sense of direction.* By forging a vision and path forward, you give people hope and unleash energy. These are the foundations for innovation and sustainable high performance.

- *Integrity lets people know that they are expected to give their best for the greater good, and that they can trust others to do the same.* When you lead with integrity, people know they can depend on you to connect them to the whole. Your example sets a standard for others to follow.

As Figure 2-1 indicates, these Five Core Strategies together enable you to mobilize creative potential and turn it into positive power—to set in motion positive ripples of confidence, energy, enthusiasm, and performance—to make a positive difference in the world.

Figure 2-1 shows the relationship between positive power and positive results

FIGURE 2-1

GETTING POSITIVE RESULTS WITH
APPRECIATIVE LEADERSHIP

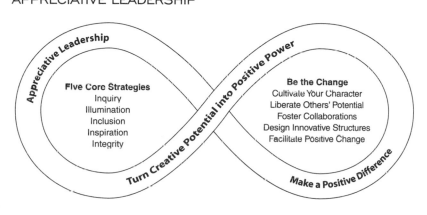

In our experience, successful Appreciative Leadership requires one to exercise all of the Five Core Strategies. Together, the strategies enable you to focus on what works, create an environment for elevated performance, and build a thriving organization. The following chapters illustrate with stories, examples, and even step-by-step directions the good news: that there are many and varied practices, tools, and methods for carrying out each of the Five Core Strategies.

THREE

The Wisdom of Inquiry: Leading with Positively Powerful Questions

THE QUESTION THAT CONNECTS US

The vice president of human resources for a regional health system arrived at the airport. She was there to give the opening speech at a community-wide meeting on health care. She had been told that the members of the community she was visiting did not see themselves as one community, and that the townspeople, farmers, and indigenous tribal members all had very different views about what health care services were most needed and why. She wondered how she might help them come together.

She was met and welcomed by a leader of the local indigenous tribe. As he drove her to town, he pointed out many beautiful natural landmarks and described their significance. Approaching a bridge across the local river, the VP said, "Tell me about the river that connects you." He responded, "You mean the river that divides us." Realizing that she had unknowingly tapped into the core story of the community, she said, "No, I mean the river that connects you." He did not respond.

The next morning, when the VP entered the conference room where she was to speak, she found him waiting. He asked if he might say a few words to the group before she began. She said, yes of course. Knowing that he was a respected leader, she was somewhat nervous about what he would say.

He began by telling the story of the car ride to town. And then he said, "She asked me a very wise question. I was so set in my ways that I didn't want to answer her question. It made me think differently about a lot of things. Last night I realized that she was right. We all need to think differently. We all need to talk about the river that connects us. I want to thank her for the wisdom of her question and welcome her to our community."

Appreciative questions are a ready source of positive power. All you have to do is ask, and a wealth of information, ideas, and knowledge unfolds. Positive questions are keys to treasure troves of best practices, success stories, and creativity. They unlock positive emotions essential to high performance such as acceptance, validation, job satisfaction, confidence, and courage. Positive questions are among Appreciative Leadership's most powerful tools. They are compelling vehicles for empowerment, for fostering risk taking, and for guiding value-based performance. They stimulate learning, change, and innovation.

Learning comes from questioning, wondering, observing, and studying: What really makes customers happy? Why do people want to work here? What kinds of relationships endure? How do great teams get started? What are my strengths as a leader? How can we get the most cost-effective results? Knowledge is created and skills are built by the questions we ask: How do you close a sale? What is the most efficiently customer-centered way to organize a distribution center? What makes a successful large-scale meeting?

Appreciative leaders develop a habit of asking positive questions to learn how people and things work when they are at their best. Their positive questions lead to a domino effect of positive outcomes: curiosity, learning, elevated respect for differences, deepened relationships, and change for the better.

The wisdom of inquiry lies with the willingness and ability to ask questions that break the mold and challenge the status quo while at the same time, strengthen relatedness and guide people to values-based performance and higher levels of consciousness. Inquiry requires daily practice: to ask more and tell less; to study the root causes of success rather than the root causes of failure; and to wonder why people do what they do, rather than judge or berate them. Appreciative leaders choose to ask about, care for, and celebrate what works well now, and they trust that by doing so, good things—what they want at work and in their life—will emerge.

Ask More and Tell Less

IF WE WERE MEANT TO TALK MORE AND LISTEN LESS,
WE WOULD HAVE TWO MOUTHS AND ONE EAR.
—MARK TWAIN

Over and over again people have told us that the best leaders they know—and the people they happily follow—are people who ask questions and truly listen to what others have to say. Consider two crews of subcontractors working on home renovations. The first crew arrives and waits for the project leader to show up. When he does, they gather, and he tells everyone what to do. He departs, and they get to work mumbling to each other things the client does not want to hear. When something unexpected happens, they stop working, call the project leader, and wait for him to return and decide what to do. The job gets done without a sense of ownership and pride. The client wonders about quality and hopes she never needs to call them back.

The second crew, in appreciative contrast, arrives on the job together. They have driven together to save gas and build camaraderie. They begin with a meeting. The project leader presents what needs to be accomplished for the day, or the week ahead, and asks: "How shall we organize to do the job? Where shall we start?" He and the team listen to each other as they discuss who will do what, the order of the work, and its relationship to everything else that is being done on the job. Within 10 minutes they have a plan and get to work. As the crew members work throughout the day, they check with each other and the client, always asking, "Is there anything else you see that we need to do?" And they do it. The client appreciates the ease with which she can discuss things with them and feels assured of the quality of their work.

As these stories show, people get engaged and feel empowered when they are *asked* to contribute rather than be told what to do. We call this the ask-to-tell ratio. Appreciative leaders ask more than they tell. Here are five ways you can increase your ask-to-tell ratio:

1. Get staff meetings off to a positive start by asking staff members to share stories of their best day at work in the past month.
2. Identify team strengths by asking team members to tell about when they were at their best as a team. Ask them to describe what makes them a great team.
3. Do a positive project debrief by asking about the "root causes of success." Ask to hear about everything that happened that make it a successful project.
4. Learn how to be a better leader by asking people to tell you what makes someone a great leader, worthy of being followed.
5. Build stronger relationships by asking people what made them happy over the weekend or on their day off.

There is never a bad time to ask a question and boost your ask-to-tell ratio. We have a colleague who is especially good at asking questions. He must have a 10-to-1 ask-to-tell ratio. He even answers questions with a question. When presented with a question, he says something like, "That's a good question, and I will answer it, but before I do, I am curious to know what *you* think?" What he finds is that 90 percent of the time when people ask a question, they actually have ideas waiting to be shared. And when given an opportunity, they easily answer their own question. He says it even works with his teenagers! Give it a try.

 What is your *ask-to-tell ratio*? Do you ask questions at least three times more than you tell people what to do or give advice? Write down two things you will do this week to increase your ask-to-tell ratio.

Questions Are Fateful

The questions we ask are fateful. They determine what we learn, and they help us create more of that which we consider to be good, true, and real. Appreciative leaders set the agenda for conversation, learning, and action through the questions they ask. Imagine a leader whose daily question is, "How did we miss that sale?" Or another who asks, "How did we reduce costs on that product?" Each question contains a topic for consideration. One invites thoughts about how to miss a sale, the other about how to reduce costs. Which would you rather have the people talking about in your organization?

Let us show you how this works. Suppose that you are very interested in reducing stress in the workplace. As part of your plan, you hire a consultant to study the situation by interviewing your team about incidents and causes of stress. One by one they are interviewed and invited to tell stories of stress, times when they experienced so much stress at work that it got in the way of their performance and perhaps even negatively impacted their health. As they recall their most stressful situations and describe them, their voice trembles, their heart rate speeds up, they flush, and they feel stressed. The consultant's question about stress has influenced what people remember, what they talk about, and how they feel. But it does not stop there. After their interviews, as team members engage in informal conversations with one another, they ask, "How did your interview go?" Once again, they retell their stories of stress in the workplace and reexperience the somatic tension. By this time they are in full agreement that there is a lot of stress in their workplace, and even the interview process was stressful!

Your topic of study—in this case, "stress in the workplace"—influenced what people recalled, how they felt, and what they talked about with each other. This is what we call the *inner dialogue of the organization*. Imagine now the memories, the stories, the lingering feelings, and the relational bonds that might form if, instead, you were interested in and chose to study "joyful productivity."

Appreciative leaders choose the topics of their questions carefully and strategically. Recognizing that the questions they ask are fateful, they use questions to set the agenda for formal and informal conversations throughout the organization. On a daily basis, the topics they choose and the questions they ask invite members of their organization to focus upon, talk about, learn about, and act on best practices, strengths, and successes.

Remember: what you ask about is what people learn about; what people learn about is what they know; what they know is what they can do. Powerful questions lead to powerful performance.

Put Your Values in Your Questions

As you have learned, appreciative questions are directed questions. They are not neutral. They are purposefully focused on what you want yourself and others to learn about and do well. They are tools for learning and performance management. The simplest and most productive way to direct your appreciative questions—and in turn, the learning and performance of people around you—is to base them on your core leadership values. For example, Amanda gets great satisfaction and truly values *helping people learn*. This leadership core value calls forth her strengths as a teacher and coach. While she is able to effectively work alone, she gets much less satisfaction doing so than when she is able to help others build capacity.

Ralph is another example of how core leadership values create a platform for the application of strengths. His core leadership values include a bias for action. When a situation requires action, his strengths go to work. He scopes out a path forward, and he creates draft plans, documents, and workshop materials. He solicits input from a wide range of people, and then he finds the people who are needed to get the job done. He values and gets great satisfaction in *making things happen*; and he is good at doing so. People follow him because it is clear what he expects for success: results!

 What three to four things do you stand for as a leader? What matters most to you? To discover your core leadership values, reflect upon the past few weeks or months at work and answer these questions:

- What gives you the most satisfaction at work?
- When do you feel good about your work?
- What are others able to do as a result of your leadership?
- What do you value most about yourself as a leader?
- Why do people respect you as a leader?

Now review your answers and identify the three or four values that are embedded in them. They are the qualities, attributes, or characteristics of work that you most value as a leader. They are what you stand for as a leader, the reasons others follow you, what gives you satisfaction at work, and what enables you to fully apply your strengths.

Once you have discovered your core leadership values, you can use them as your expectations for excellence. They can serve as your measures of a job well done. The people we talked with repeatedly said that effective leaders—the people they want to follow—clearly communicate what they expect, and they consistently recognize people for meeting those expectations. Appreciative leaders convey expectations and provide direction by putting their values into questions that direct the thinking and action of those with whom they work. A warehouse manager told us how she put her core value of "creativity" into a question she asked her team:

> Sales had been especially good, and the warehouse had three times as much merchandise to deliver the following week than usual. Rather than making a decision and telling the team what to do, I gathered them together, described the challenge, and asked them a question: "What creative ideas do you have for how we might handle this situation?" Responses were both creative and practical: "I'll work all seven days next week." "We could all work on Sunday and then have dinner together." "We could hire a moving company." "Some of our teenage sons might want to help out for the week." I was amazed by people's creativity and commitment! By their responses I also learned how family oriented they all were.

When sharing her story with us, this woman said, "It works. If you ask for what you want, you really can get it." Not only did the following week go smoothly. It also elevated the team to a new level of performance in which they regularly enjoyed helping each other find new and creative ways to do their work. What was the team's reward for their job well done? They were given the opportunity to discuss—and the budget to act on—another value-based question: "How might we creatively engage our families in celebration of our success?" As this story shows, appreciative leaders express what is important to them and guide people's thinking, dialogue, and performance by asking value-based questions.

In the language of Appreciative Inquiry, your core leadership values are the best topics for your questions. If you value cost savings, ask people to tell you and each other about times when they saved money. Ask them how they did it, why they did it, and how it felt to do so. If you value collaboration, ask people about times of unprecedented collaboration, times when they were surprised by the goodness in people and their capacity to collaborate. If you value hospitality in customer service, ask about it. Seek to understand what hospitality means to people of different cultures. The more you ask questions based on your core leadership values, the more clearly others will know what you stand for as a leader and the more you and others will learn how to bring those values to life.

Remember: the best way to convey your values is to put them into your questions. The Appreciative Leadership mantra is, "Ask more, tell less."

The Flip

THE BEST LEADERS ASK QUESTIONS THAT OTHERS AREN'T ASKING.

Appreciative leaders are highly skilled at turning negative issues into positive questions. In other words, they know how to do *The Flip*. The Appreciative Inquiry Positive Principle suggests that the more positive the questions we ask, the more positive and enduring the change.[1] Very often when change is needed, people describe that need as a problem, something they do not want, or something that has undesired consequences. When people feel stuck in the midst of an unsatisfactory situation over a period of time, all they know how to do is complain about it. Appreciative leaders, however, have what Thatchenkery and Metzker call "Appreciative Intelligence": the capacity to see the implicit positive potential in a situation.[2] They are able to see positive potential, and they invite it to come to life by asking positive questions. The following example shows The Flip in action.

Diana was on a conference call with the chairman of the board of an international professional association. She listened as he listed problem after problem: staff members are critical of each other and of members; there is little collaboration among staff and board members; no one is willing to go the extra mile; everyone complains about the cost of membership; members seldom volunteer to serve on committees or to write articles for the newsletter. The list of problems went on and on. Diana gently interrupted the habitual tirade:

Diana: May I share my reflections and ask a question?

Peter: Yes.

Diana: I hear that you are very frustrated and feeling somewhat overwhelmed with all the problems people bring to you.

Peter: Yes.

Diana: I wonder what it is that you really want. You have described in detail what you do not want—all the problems. I am curious, what do you want for the association, its members, and the board and the staff?

Peter: That is quite easy. I would like more members who are actively engaged.

Diana: That is a clear and exciting image for the future. I suggest that you begin an inquiry into "Engaged Membership." Ask members of the board, the staff, and the association to share stories of when they have been highly engaged as members of the association and/or as members of another organization, team, or community. Ask them who or what led them to be so engaged. What did they do and contribute? How did leadership encourage and support their engagement? How did it feel? What were the benefits to them and to others? What ideas do they have to enhance engaged membership in the association?

Peter: That is a very different approach.

Diana: Yes, when you flip problems and ask about what you really want, two things happen. One, people learn what it is that you stand for as a leader. They learn what you expect of them. In your case it is "Engaged Membership." And two, you get more of want you want. When people know what is wanted and expected for success, they do it.

As Diana demonstrated, The Flip is a way to turn critical comments, frustrating issues, and problems into affirmative questions. It is as simple as 1, 2, 3:

1. When presented with a complaint or a problem, listen carefully. Repeat what was said to be sure both that you understand it and that the other person feels heard.
2. Ask, "What is it that you really want? I understand that you are not happy with the way things are, but tell me what is it that you want instead?"
3. Reflect what you heard—The Flip. Describe what the person really wants in a two- or three-word phrase—an affirmative topic.

Key to a successful flip is the question: "What do you really want?" We suggest that you practice asking it of yourself, as well as asking it of others. The more you practice this, the clearer you and others will become about what it is that you really do want, and the easier it will be to learn, change, and create the work and personal life in that image.

You may be thinking, "Sure, this is great, but what about the cynic who just complains and complains?" It seems that every work group has at least one. Consultant Peter Lange reminds his clients that "behind every cynical statement is a dream wanting to be expressed." He explains that when people are being cynical or critical, they are comparing the current situation with an ideal—something they have seen, heard, or imagined. He suggests that the best way to respond to a cynical or critical statement is to first acknowledge that the situation is less than ideal and then to ask for a description of the ideal—what the situation would be like if it were the best it could be. In essence, what Peter is suggesting is to do The Flip by acknowledging what is and then inquiring into the ideal as an appreciative alternative.

In our work we often come across what we call *habitual problems*. They are issues that are discussed as problems over and over again, using the same vocabularies and metaphors, in organization after organization. In most cases, a great deal of time and energy is spent talking about and studying these problems—they are habits embedded in the organization's ways of thinking, talking, and working. They are ripe for The Flip.

Several of these habitual problems, along with appreciative alternatives (that is, affirmative topics), are listed in Table 3-1. Use these as samples when you are practicing The Flip.

TABLE 3-1
THE FLIP

Habitual Problems	Possible Affirmative Topics
Employee turnover	Employee retention
	Magnetic work environment
Low test scores	Successful learning
	Good study habits
Too little time	When saying "no" is the answer
	Working in the flow
Work group silos	Productive collaboration
	Teamwork across lines
Technology breakdowns	Technology that serves
	Users as designers

When we invite groups to flip from problem talk to an appreciative alternative, The Flip often comes easily. And once they flip their thinking and inquiry from habitual problems to affirmative topics, positive change occurs in a myriad of remarkable ways, as seen in the following examples:

- A Mexican manufacturing company, plagued by a culture in which women mainly worked on the front lines and wielded little influence, flipped its attention from sexual harassment to positive cross-gender relationships. In so doing, it came to be acknowledged by the Catalyst Foundation in 1997 as the best company in Mexico for women to work in.[3]

- A major hospital system was faced with countless challenges in the areas of nurse staffing and workload. When they flipped their attention from nursing turnover to explore why nurses stayed in their system, their statistics after one year were stunning: nurse retention increased by 13 percent; vacancy rates decreased by 30 percent; nurses' rating the hospital as a good place to work increased by 16 percent; and patient satisfaction with nursing (as measured by the Press Ganey survey) increased by 20 points.[4]

- A global high-tech giant was challenged by radically increased competition. When they flipped their attention from their diminishing market share to forging a culture that would ensure their ongoing leadership, employees were inspired and motivated to action. Business revenues rose from $26 million to $30 million over a three-year period, in the face of intensely increased competition.

- Faced with a projected $70 million budget shortfall, a municipal government flipped its attention to explore what it would take for it to thrive in challenging times. In the process, they increased employee commitment to controversial cost-saving initiatives, developed a new incentive retirement program, and generated grassroots ideas that enabled them to consolidate services and facilities.

Now it is your turn to practice The Flip. Take a few minutes and use Table 3-2 as a template for recording and transforming some of your organization's or community's habitual problems.

First, list two or three habitual problems in column 1: the challenges, issues, or frustrations that your organization or community talks about over and over again.

Second, ask yourself the question, "What is it that we really want more of in our organization or community?" Record these reflections in column 2.

Third, ask yourself, "When we are at our best, what is it that makes us uniquely who we are?" Record these ideas in column 3.

Finally, circle the one or two reflections that excite you as potential appreciative topics for future inquiry and action. In doing this, you may notice, as many people do, that what you really want in your organization or community is to be more like who you are at your best. This is a wonderful discovery!

TABLE 3-2 FLIPPING HABITUAL PROBLEMS INTO AFFIRMATIVE TOPICS		
	Possible Affirmative Topics	
1. Habitual Problems	2. What Do We Really Want?	2. When Are We At Our Best?

The Flip can be an individual activity—as you just did it—or it can be done by a group of people, a team, or department. Because our organizational realities are created in conversations among many different people, we strongly suggest that you gather your team or a cross-department group and guide them through The Flip. They will appreciate being asked to participate in such a positive and strategic process. And together you will begin the journey of creating a new organizational or community reality.

The Anatomy of an Appreciative Inquiry Question

Appreciative leaders are versed in the skills of crafting and asking appreciative questions. Their ability to ask great questions depends on their ability to craft great questions. The qualities of appreciative questions are illustrated in the many examples throughout this book. They are unconditionally positive. They evoke stories rather than lists of ideas. They are open-ended—yet at the same time, they probe into specific causes of success. Most importantly, they are sincere requests to understand the topic being considered from the perspectives of the people being asked the questions.

Table 3-3 describes the three parts of a great appreciative question, together with examples—taken from a health care setting—for each of the three parts. Use this as a model for crafting your own appreciative questions.

Each of the three parts of an appreciative question is important:

- The *affirmative topic* sets the stage. It says, "This is what is important for us to learn about and to act upon." It conveys your core leadership value.
- The *lead-in* then conveys confidence that we have experienced the topic. It invites us to draw on our experiences. It is an implicit validation of the person being interviewed. It sets the tone of the interview as an open and sincere invitation to tell a story.
- The *string of probes* invites a deep dive into the causes of success. Together they provide insight into the specifics of the story: who did what, and how the success was created.

TABLE 3-3
THREE PARTS OF GREAT APPRECIATIVE QUESTIONS

Part 1. *Value-based affirmative topic:* A two- to four-word phrase that says what you value and want more of in your team or organization. It is the key idea or issue you intend to study, learn about, and more fully put into action.

Example: Collaborative patient-centered care.

Part 2. *Rapport-building lead-in:* A three- to four-sentence paragraph that explains what the topic means and why it is important. It assumes that the topic occurs and has been experienced when the organization or community is at its best. It states what the question is focused on and seeks a story about a high-point experience of the chosen affirmative topic.

Example: Delivering quality patient care requires collaboration among a wide range of care providers. When we are at our best, we all focus on patient-centered care. This means we support each other to have the time to talk to and listen to our patients and their families. We give them options and the information they need to make informed decisions. And most of all, we care. Tell me about a time when you were part of a team that provided high-quality, patient-centered care.

Part 3. *A string of empowering probes:* Questions that probe into the specifics of the high-point story and the causes of its success. They ask about who was involved and what they did to contribute to the high-point experience. They may ask about benefits to various people involved. They often ask about actions and feelings.

Examples:

- What was the situation?
- Who else was involved, and what did they do to ensure collaborative patient-centered care?
- What was your role, and how did you foster collaboration?
- How did you feel?
- How did the patient benefit from this collaboration?
- What can we learn from this situation to ensure that we consistently collaborate for the well-being of our patients?

Together the three parts of an appreciative question establish focus, build rapport, and identify results-oriented patterns of success.

To learn more about how to craft Appreciative Inquiry questions, we suggest you read *The Power of Appreciative Inquiry*. This book provides a clear overview of the Appreciative Inquiry process in action, along with a bevy of practical and useful tools for applying Appreciative Inquiry in organization and community settings.

Inquiry: The Fast Track to Engagement, Risk Taking, and Results

Inquiry is the most direct, simplest, and fastest way to foster engagement and generate responsibility for the future. Asking a question is an act of engagement. Listening to people's ideas and opinions validates people, supporting the only real kind of empowerment—self-empowerment. When leaders discover and affirm people's strengths and potential contributions, they demonstrate confidence and inspire self-responsibility. When asked to share their ideas and opinions, people get engaged and commit to action. The more that people are invited to contribute their thoughts, ideas, and opinions, the more they will contribute both actions and results. Asking leads to action. Leading with positively powerful questions is a way to accelerate engagement and energize teams, departments, and whole organizations to make a positive difference.

In our work as executive coaches, we frequently hear frustration about the lack of engagement and responsibility in organizations. Executives spend significant amounts of money on employee engagement surveys, only to learn what they already knew: that their workforce is neither engaged in nor committed to the organization and its goals, strategy, and leadership. When we ask these executives what they have been doing to stimulate engagement, we often discover that they have been preaching rather than practicing engagement.

Telling adults what to do does not motivate them. Telling people to be empowered, to take ownership, to be responsible, or to have accountability does not work. In fact, more often than not, it has the exact opposite effect. Over and over again, the people we interviewed said that the leaders they choose to follow are people who "walk the talk," and whose audio and video match. They said that people who do not practice what they preach are not real leaders, no matter what their job titles may be.

This is not new. People want leaders who "walk the talk." So what does this have to do with inquiry? The quickest and most authentic way to engage people and build a sense of responsibility is to ask them to share their thoughts, feelings, and ideas. Appreciative leaders use inquiry to engage people's hearts and minds, to draw out and listen to their innovative ideas, and to give them confidence to trust their own intuition and take risks for a better future.

As the following story shows, there is a direct link between inquiry, engagement, risk taking, and positive results:

When I became dean of the college, it was losing money. Soon after accepting the position, I announced that I would not cut one penny from the budget. Upon hearing this pronouncement, two of my advisors immediately scheduled meetings with me. The first began and ended our meeting telling me that the only viable option was to cut the budget. He presented clear reasons why budget cuts were necessary, acknowledging that to so do would demoralize faculty and staff but reinforcing that it was the only way. He said nothing to give me hope for the future or to make me glad to have taken the job—nor did he ask me what I was thinking.

Fortunately, the next day's meeting was a totally different experience. It began and ended with sincere inquiry. My second advisor opened by saying that she was curious and wanted to understand my decision not to cut the budget. She was calm and didn't say much—but she asked a lot of questions. And she listened. "What about the college leads you to think that we can save money without cutting the budget? When have you taken such a big risk and had it pay off? Tell me about the situation? How do you imagine getting the faculty and staff engaged in your campaign to cut costs? What ideas do you have for raising money? Whom do you plan to involve in helping to raise funds? What is your greatest hope for your first year here? What support do you need? How can I best help you?" Her questions were affirming. They helped me make connections and think deeper than I had up until that point.

As she shared the story with us, the dean described this advisor's style as a calming influence: a powerful kind of leadership that encouraged her to trust herself and take the risk she knew was right. The results? The new dean kept her word. She did not cut the budget. And in her first year as dean, the college broke even! Most significantly, she learned from experience about the positive power of leading with questions.

Inquiry is a valuable leadership resource, available to all levels of an organization. It can be used to help one person think through ideas, create a path forward, and commit to a risk-taking course of action. Or it can be used as a fast track to engage an entire team, department, or organization in new ways of working.

Appreciatively:
Who, What, Where, When, and *How* Questions

Appreciative leaders ask positive variations of the familiar *who, what, where, when,* and *how* questions. The questions they ask seek fully affirmative descriptions and stories. Appreciative leaders flip questions about problems to questions about success, opportunities, and potential. When they ask why something happened, it is to shed light on why it was successful. In these cases they quickly turn *why* into "Who, what, where, when, and how was it successful?" Table 3-4 shows negative and positive variations of *who, what, where, when*, and *how* questions. They are categorically different questions. First, read the column of negative questions on the left. What do you think of as you read them? How do you feel? Are they familiar to you? Now, read the column of positive questions on the right. What do you think about and recall as you read them? How do they make you feel?

Always focusing on positive possibilities, appreciative leaders use *who, what, where, when*, and *how* questions to uncover strengths, hopes, and dreams. They ask them to discover who needs to be involved in a situation, and where or how to go forward in order to ensure desired outcomes. Consider the following examples:

- *When* were you at your best?
- Tell me about a high-point experience *when* you were at your best doing [your value-based affirmative topic].

TABLE 3-4
VARIATIONS IN *WHO, WHAT, WHERE, WHEN,* AND *HOW* QUESTIONS

	Negative Variations	Positive Variations
Who	*Who* was involved in creating this situation?	*Who* else was involved, and *what* did he or she contribute to the success?
What	*What* went wrong to cause this problem?	*What* can we do to make a positive impact?
Where	*Where* are the biggest gaps in our strategy?	*Where* are the opportunities to leverage our strengths?
When	*When* did this happen?	*When* have we been at our best?
How	*How* did we let this happen?	*How* can we collaborate to get the results we all want?

- Tell me about a time *when* you have felt satisfaction and pride in your work.
- Tell me about a time, a situation, or a position *when* you were most engaged, alive, and energized at work.

When questions, like those above are great sources of stories about strengths. If you want to learn about a person's high-performance patterns, ask a *when* question. Listen to the person's answer, and draw out strengths and high performance patterns.

- *Who* else needs to be involved in order for us to succeed in the future?
- *Who* else has a stake in the future we are creating?
- *Who* needs to be involved because they will be impacted by what we are planning?
- *Who* can we learn from?
- *Who* has strengths that best complement your strengths?

Who questions, as those above show, are essential building blocks for effective work relationships. They are key resources for ensuring that all the people whose future it is are included in the conversations and decision making. If you want to ensure that you have commitment, be sure to ask who needs to be involved in order to make the decisions and carry them out.

- *What* are your wildest hopes and dreams for [the organization, your career, the future, our team, your new book, and so on]?
- If you had three wishes to improve the health and vitality of [our workplace, the community, the organization, our department or team, our family, our relationship, and so on], *what* would they be?
- *What* would you do if you were in charge?

What questions are windows to the future. They are an effective way to generate possibilities, explore options, and unlock potential. If you want to stimulate creativity and uncover opportunities for innovation, ask what is possible, what might happen, what could be better, what are your boldest and most compelling hopes and dreams?

- *Where* are the greatest opportunities to realize our hopes and dreams?
- *Where* might we leverage our strengths for even better results?
- *Where* shall we begin?

Where questions are strategic divining rods. They bring general ideas to life by identifying specific areas for action. If you want to focus action, ask where are the biggest opportunities, where are the openings for collaboration, where shall we start to ensure a long-lasting impact?

- *How* shall we proceed?
- *How* can I help you realize your wildest hopes and dreams?
- *How* can I support you right now?

How questions, like those above, create the path forward together. They are process questions. They tell us who will do what by when. They provide information about actions, support, and resources needed. If you want to get people in alignment about next steps, ask, discuss, and determine how. How shall we organize to achieve our goals? How shall we engage others? How shall we communicate our intention? How shall we measure and celebrate our success?

Obviously, there are an endless number of appreciative questions available at any given time. They are a powerful resource that will never run out. Ask one; and if you like it, ask it again. You may find a few that are your regulars. Or you may find that you like the creative process of making up new questions as new situations emerge.

Consider starting a question log or journal. Record the questions you ask and the responses you get. You may even want to record changes you see in people as you consistently ask them positively powerful questions. Keep your log or journal for 30 days, and then make note of the changes you see and feel in yourself and your relationships at work and at home. Make note of your favorite and most powerful questions.

Team Inquiry and Team Performance

Teams, like people, learn, grow, and move in the direction of what they study. This makes inquiry a very powerful strategy for team development. A team's stage of development can be defined by the questions it needs to ask. You can foster team development and team performance by gathering team members and asking the following stage-appropriate questions.

In the Beginning

When people gather to form a team, their initial curiosities are about getting to know each other and exploring who they are as a group on the path to becoming a team. Helpful questions include these:

- *Who* are we, individually and collectively?
- *What* are our strengths, values, and capacities, individually and collectively?
- *What* energizes us, individually and collectively?

When these questions are addressed, the group moves from being a collection of individuals to a team with a collective identity and voice—"we."

Clarifying Goals and Roles

As people are getting to know one another and building their team identity, the issues of who is doing what and why surfaces. Helpful questions at this phase of team development include these:

- *Why* is our task, goal, or issue important to you?
- *What* is your vision for our success?
- *What* about our work inspires you to give your best?
- *How* do you see yourself contributing?

When these questions are posed and successfully discussed, the team gains clarity about its purpose, goals, and roles—who will do what, with whom, and by when.

Learning to Work with Differences

Every team goes through a phase of needing to learn to respect differences. Few teams begin by truly understanding how different members think, feel, and work. As these differences emerge in the life of a team, they can be put to good use with questions such as these:

- *What* do you most value and respect about the way we work as a team?
- *What* do you bring to us that no one else on the team can bring?
- *How* have you successfully resolved differences of opinion in the past?
- *What* are some of the best practices you have experienced or heard about for teams to learn to work with differences of opinion?

When these questions, or others that are similar in intent, are addressed, trust, respect, and hope emerge. The team is really ready to get to work!

Fostering High Performance

Relationships are formed, goals and roles are clear, and differences are respected. In other words, the team foundation is in place for high performance. Yet even at this point there are questions. Consider these:

- Tell me about a team that brought out your best; *how* did it do this?
- *What* is your image of us as a high-performing team?
- Based on your knowledge of other successful teams, *what* principles guide high-performance teams?
- *How* shall we celebrate our successes?

When teams use inquiry to identify shared principles of high performance and ways to celebrate success, they skyrocket to success. They become what they study: a high-performing team.

Growing from Success

There is a time in the life of every team to pause and to reflect on the way the team members are working together and with others. Unfortunately, too many teams do this only in the face of problems, barriers, or failures. Appreciative Leadership guides high-performing teams to use inquiry as a way to grow from success. Helpful questions at this time in a team's life include these:

- *What* was the high point of the process or project for you?
- *Who* or *what* made this a successful endeavor for you? *How?*
- *What* can we learn from this situation to ensure our ongoing success?
- If you were to give us an award, *what* would it be for, and *what* would it be?

When teams take time to study and learn from their successes and best practices, team members feel appreciated and the team furthers its knowledge and collective wisdom. Team members get an opportunity for reflection and renewal that can help them confidently commit to the team's next endeavor.

By engaging with one another through inquiry, team members create a foundation of trust, respect, and confidence. They develop the relational capacity and resiliency to face the future—uncertain though it may be. Take, for example, the team formed to guide a manufacturing company's migration from one information system to another. Recognizing the magnitude and importance of the task, many of the team members came to it with anxiety. Few believed that they were the right people for the job. Their first meeting began with inquiry. In pairs, people explored times when they had heard about or participated in a significant change initiative that had gone exceptionally well. They inquired into one another's unique strengths, skills, and talents—the things that each of them brought to the team, in service of positive change. And finally, they gathered one another's hopes and dreams for the organization—all the ways in which this initiative would pave the way for a positive future.

Had we made "before" and "after" videos of their interviews, they would have looked like two different teams. The inquiry not only provided information for them to know what to do; it also gave them confidence and assurance that they were the right ones to do it. The plans they formed following this inquiry were grounded in experience, wisdom, and inspiration. The ultimate result was an on-time, underbudget system implementation.

Building Bridges with Inquiry

Whatever the divide in your organization or community, it can be bridged with inquiry. When people from different departments, functions, levels, ages, genders, and/or cultures interview each other, relationships are formed and collaboration unfolds naturally. Inquiry is a silo buster. It gives people who need to (but don't) work together a way to come together and learn about and from each other. In so doing, they see the potential benefits of collaboration and realize there is more to gain than to lose.

In preparation for a divisionwide strategic planning process, we asked the four business units at the Hunter Douglas Window Fashions Division to each study a sister business unit. The task was to conduct inquiry into the achievements and root causes of success of their assigned organization. They were to come to the strategic planning meeting prepared to share what they had learned and present their assigned business unit with an award. For three weeks before the meeting, cross–business unit interviews were conducted, stories and data were analyzed, and presentations were prepared. The meeting began with each business unit's hearing the presentation of another describing the following:

- Their greatest achievements in the past three years
- How they have contributed to the division's overall success
- What makes others proud to be part of their sister business unit
- What others have learned from them
- The greatest potential for the future of their business

These *success-oriented status reports* were then followed by the awards ceremony. Each business unit received its award along with a creative description of why it was deserved. It was a fun way to foster interorganizational collaboration and cross-unit learning, while generating the status reports that would serve as a foundation for the organization's strategic planning. The meeting's beginning high led to some of the most creative planning ever done in the division. New product ideas were born along with new marketing strategies that over time radically enhanced an already successful business.

Time after time we find that inquiry among improbable pairs of departments, functions, or whole organizations builds relationships and fosters collaboration. We have used Appreciative Inquiry to support merger integration, to envision, design, and lead a global interfaith organization, and to enhance union/management partnerships. Whenever you sense a need to build bridges among people, groups, or organizations, give inquiry a chance. Frame an appreciative question that transcends the divide, and invite improbable pairs to interview each other. You will be amazed by the amount of commonality previously estranged people discover. You will be amazed by the spontaneous restoration of relationships that occurs. And you will be amazed by the ease with which collaboration emerges.

Creating a Culture of Inquiry

Appreciative Leadership fosters a culture of full-voice, high-engagement inquiry. Meetings begin with positive questions. Analysis of the root causes of success is the norm. All stakeholders are regularly invited to participate in the Appreciative Inquiry processes of strategic significance. Affirmative topics are chosen such as first to market, green product development, sustainable manufacturing, health care reform, or collaborative advantage. And once the topics are selected, hundreds or even thousands of people participate in the Appreciative Inquiry 4-D process:

- *Discovery:* Together they identify strengths and core competencies, and they "map the organization's positive core."
- *Dream:* They collectively envision positive possibilities for the future, articulate a shared vision, and select strategic opportunities to focus on.
- *Design:* They create aspiration statements for each opportunity and design the processes and structures needed to achieve them.
- *Destiny:* They scope out a collaborative path forward and make personal commitments to contribute their strengths and resources to realize their shared aspirations.

By championing organization-wide inquiry on topics of strategic significance, Appreciative Leadership sets learning and innovation in motion. By inviting and including all of the organization's stakeholders, appreciative leaders ensure that the knowledge, ways of working, and aspirations that are generated are meaningful to everyone.

Enhancing Your Capacity:
Resources for Further Development

TABLE 3-5		
INQUIRY: A SUMMARY OF KEY PRACTICES		
	Key Practices	**Page Numbers**
Personal	• Boost your ask-to-tell ratio.	29
	• Practice The Flip.	35
One-to-one	• Ask value-based questions.	32
Team or group	• Engage in team inquiry.	49
	• Prepare success-oriented status reports.	53
Whole organization or community	• Create a culture of inquiry.	54

Recommended Books

Appreciative Team Building by Diana Whitney, Amanda Trosten-Bloom, Jay Cherney, and Ron Fry (New York, London, Shanghai: iUniverse), 2004.

Change Your Questions, Change Your Life, by Marilee G. Adams (San Francisco: Berrett-Koehler), 2004.

Encyclopedia of Positive Questions by Diana Whitney, David L. Cooperrider, Amanda Trosten-Bloom, and Brian S. Kaplin (Brunswick, OH: Crown Custom Publishing), 2005.

The Power of Appreciative Inquiry, 2nd ed., by Diana Whitney and Amanda Trosten-Bloom (San Francisco: Berrett-Kohler), 2010.

Recommended Web Sites

Appreciative Inquiry Commons

http://appreciativeinquiry.case.edu

The Appreciative Inquiry Commons is a worldwide portal hosted by Case Western Reserve University's Weatherhead School of Management. Devoted to sharing academic resources and practical tools on Appreciative Inquiry and the rapidly growing discipline of positive change.

Corporation for Positive Change

www.positivechange.org

Corporation for Positive Change is the premier consulting firm using Appreciative Inquiry for transformation and innovation in business, government, and nonprofit organizations around the world. This is the authors' Web site.

The Inquiry Institute

www.inquiryinstitute.com

The Inquiry Institute helps people "strengthen their inquiring mindsets" to facilitate success in their professional and personal lives.

FOUR

The Art of Illumination: Bringing out the Best of People and Situations

TEN MINUTES OF ILLUMINATION

The president of the R&D division of a major pharmaceutical company was welcoming 400 people to the company's annual leadership conference. She was to speak for 10 minutes and then introduce me as the keynote speaker. Not knowing her well, I worried that she might spend her full 10 minutes listing all the reasons why this group of exceptionally talented people needed leadership development. That she might flood them with problems and reminders of inadequacy, the way I have seen all too many executives do, to make their case for leadership development. I was surprised that she did just the opposite—in fact, so positively surprised that throughout my speech I referred to her talk as an example of "10 minutes of illumination."

What did she say and do in that 10 minutes?

She called out by name and recognized at least 20 percent of the people in the room. She described specific actions, risks, and results they had achieved. She described in detail a potentially significant scientific innovation and again named those who had created the strategy, presented it to the executive board, and secured approval and funding to move it forward. She talked about her own development as a scientist and as a leader and about how the two go hand-in-hand in her experience and practice. She named and acknowledged her mentors, coaches, and learning companions. In a short 10 minutes, she brought out the best of almost a hundred people and offered up their stories as clear and compelling models from which others might learn.

She practiced the art of illumination.

People's strengths, capabilities, needs, wants, hopes, and dreams are a readily abundant yet frequently overlooked source of positive power. Generally, unrecognized and very often underutilized, strengths are a deep well of potential waiting to be tapped. Appreciative Leadership puts strengths to work, transforming them from raw potential into positive results through the art of illumination.

Success breeds success. Stories of strengths, high performance, and best practices create momentum and pave paths forward for ongoing high performance. People want to get positive results. They listen and look to leadership to understand how to do so. Few people get up in the morning thinking, "I really want to make a lot of mistakes today." Rather, most people wonder, "What do I need to do around here to succeed?" They seek answers to that question by watching the actions of their leaders and listening to the stories they tell.

Leadership can shine the light on strengths, high-performance patterns, and root causes of success, or it can leave people in the dark wondering what is expected of them. When leaders fail to engage people in sharing stories of strengths, hope, and high performance, people are left unclear about what they must do to succeed. But when leaders discover and pass along stories of outstanding results, they are implicitly saying, "This is the way to do things around here if you too want to be a recognized winner."

The art of illumination requires the willingness and ability to see what works rather than what doesn't, the interest and capacity to discover peoples' strengths, and the capability to sense the positive potential in every person and situation. Illumination is like the sun: when it radiates, people feel it and are warmed by it—and are therefore eager to give their best. As Table 4-1 shows, there are four important illumination practices: seeking, seeing, sharing, and aligning the best of people and situations.

TABLE 4-1
FOUR PRACTICES OF ILLUMINATION

1. *Seeking the Best of People, Situations, and Organizations*

Appreciative leaders actively seek to discover the unique skills, abilities, strengths, and positive potential of every person and situation. They ask questions and use assessments to identify strengths, work style preferences, and high-performance patterns. They engage others in inquiry to uncover positive potential and people's hopes and dreams for the future. By routinely seeking the best, appreciative leaders create a powerfully positive presence that others are naturally drawn to follow.

Do you seek to understand why people succeed? Are you curious about people's unique skills, abilities, hopes, and dreams? Are you a strengths spotter?

2. *Seeing What Works When People Are at Their Best*

Appreciative leaders have their eyes and ears open to see and hear what works. They have a distinct preference for understanding specific details of why people, products, services, and processes succeed—the root causes of their success. They are always on the lookout for the best way of doing things. They argue for strengths, standardization of best practices, and inspiring innovation. They trust those who can see ahead of the curve; and they trust their intuition and wisdom about what will succeed.

(Continued)

TABLE 4-1 *(Continued)*

Do you regularly listen to success stories and analyze them to understand best practices? Do you trust intuition—your own and other people's? Do you facilitate dialogue about the root causes of success?

3. *Sharing Stories of Best Practices for Learning and Standardization*

Appreciative leaders tell stories of success. They spread best practices and give credit to the people involved. They recognize people by name and describe their accomplishments as specifically as possible. They know that the stories they tell teach others what is expected. Recognizing that words create worlds, they choose their stories and their words wisely. They set expectations for success by telling stories of success.

Do you collect success stories and share them every chance you get? Do you acknowledge high performers? Do you encourage everyone to learn and standardize processes based on stories of best practices?

4. *Aligning Strengths for Development and Collaborative Advantage*

Appreciative leaders optimize strengths by cultivating people's unique skills and talents. And they align people's strengths—providing opportunities for people do what they do well—and collaborate with others whose strengths are complementary. Recognizing that strengths combined with strengths creates collaborative advantages and gets results, they reach out to engage diverse groups of people in ways that make weaknesses irrelevant.

Do you work from your strengths and help others to do the same? Do you analyze strengths and align them when assigning work or creating teams? Do you engage diverse groups of people to optimize strengths?

From Criticism to Illumination: The Path to Retention and Results

MAKING PEOPLE FEEL VALUED MAKES THEM VALUE
YOU AND WANT TO DO MORE.

The pattern of interaction and relatedness in many organizations today is defined by criticism. People who speak out do so at the risk of prompting others—superiors and peers alike—to respond with critical and often personally demeaning comments. The result can be devastating to employees' confidence and willingness to take the risks that result in innovation, integrity, and high performance.

Consider the story of Harris, a 30-something graduate of Georgetown University, Stanford Business School, and Oxford. Just weeks from being awarded his Ph.D., he accepted a position with an international consulting firm on the promise of work that would use his skills and continue to stimulate his growth and development. Within the first month on the job, he was sent to a weeklong training program on research methods. It was a program required of all new hires—most of whom were just out of undergraduate college. When Harris would make comments or ask challenging questions, he often felt belittled by the trainer. Wondering if this program was appropriate, he approached his supervisor, only to be told that he was being "egotistical and grandiose." After three months of continuous criticism, he left the firm and entered counseling, seeking to understand what he had done wrong. The manager's criticism lost the consulting firm a valuable resource and reinforced a supervisory style of critique bordering on abuse. In addition, it led a bright young man into a downward spiral of self-doubt rather than into an upward spiral of learning and contribution.

Illumination—seeing and valuing peoples' ideas, skills, and aspirations—has a very different impact on people, as Susan's story shows. Another 30-something with a deep well of potential, and 10 years of experience in domestic and international communication strategy with an MPA from Harvard's Kennedy School, Susan applied for a position with an international nongovernmental organization (NGO). During the interview she described her long-range desire to become an executive director of an international NGO. The hiring manager, who was the current executive director of the NGO Susan was applying to, was an attentive listener and heard Susan's aspiration to diversify her experience. Recognizing her natural abilities to manage people, projects, events, and functions, and realizing that Susan would benefit by learning the development function, she offered her a job as development manager. The learning curve was steep, and yet in the first three months Susan hired three additional staff, managed the production of the annual fundraising event, and established positive relationships with staff around the world. In this case the manager took a risk to put someone with no content knowledge but superb managerial skills into a position that paid off for everyone. Her ability to see and appreciate potential set off an upward spiral of achievement and satisfaction for both the young woman and the organization.

Positive Self-Talk: The Vocabulary for Illumination

Positive power starts with the way we talk to ourselves—that is, what we say and feel about ourselves and the world around us. The more positive our self-talk, the easier it is for us to see others' strengths and successes. The practice of illumination begins by recognizing our own strengths, joys, and successes and talking about them to ourselves and others.

This may sound a bit wacky, but admit it: you talk to yourself. Most people admit to self-talk while bathing or showering, while driving or riding on buses, planes, and trains, or while being in nature, walking in the woods or sitting by water. Psychologist William James posited that every one of us has a running stream of consciousness—an inner dialogue of thoughts and feelings about our self, our relationships, our life, and our work. Self-talk is natural. But how strengths oriented is your self-talk? How success oriented is your self-talk? How *healthy* is your self-talk?

Your inner confidence manifests in how you carry yourself in the world, and your inner vocabulary is the same language you access when talking to others. Your self-talk not only influences your own health, well-being, and performance; it is also the lens through which you see and talk to others. Remember the childhood taunt "It takes one to know one"? Well, it is true. As Figure 4-1 shows, what you see and say about yourself becomes the limit of what you can see and say about others, which is an important contributor to your capacity to influence others' performance.

Leaders are always on stage being watched and listened to as role models, guides, and facilitators of other people's performance. When

FIGURE 4-1
LEADERSHIP SELF-TALK IMPACTS PERFORMANCE

people say that they want leaders who "walk the talk," they are asking for leaders who are self-aware and whose words are congruent with their actions. Leadership self-talk is mirrored outwardly, and it illuminates in others the leader's own insecurities, capabilities, hopes, and dreams.

The lesson here is simple. If you see something in someone else that is troublesome for you, change it in yourself. You must be the target of your own transformational activities in order for your team, organization, and/or community to change. On the other hand, if you see something in another that you value, respect, or admire, make it your own. Adapt it and improve it, and you will become what you most respect and admire about others. As you change, so will the world around you. And if the world doesn't, no matter! You will have become a better person and leader, regardless.

Appreciative Check-in: Group Illumination

A way to ensure that you start conversations and meetings off on a positive note is through an *appreciative check-in*. Once people are gathered but before reviewing the agenda, ask people to briefly share anything that has gone well in the past day or two. Tell them that it may be personal or work related, that ideally it is something they are proud about and/or that others can learn from by hearing it.

When first introduced to the practice of appreciative check-ins, people may be hesitant or slow to offer up their experiences. After hearing others' short stories of success and being invited repeatedly to share, they will readily do so themselves. We recently attended a meeting with a major health system. People were invited to offer up successes, joys, and celebrations of the past week. We heard about a team member's newborn child, another's "ah-ha" in having learned Appreciative Inquiry, another's excitement in having created a community garden, and finally, the launch of a new initiative in an operating room. All this appreciative news felt good to hear, created an atmosphere of openness and sharing, and taught team members about one another.

Appreciative check-ins can transform problem talk into potential talk and foster positive powerful conversations about crucial work agenda items. For years Connie began her staff meetings by asking how many incidents of inappropriate documentation had occurred that week. She believed this was the most important issue her team needed to address so she led with it. As a result every meeting started off on what she later described as a "sour note" with people actually dreading the conversation. After learning about Appreciative Inquiry, Connie changed the way she started meetings. She began with appreciative check-ins, and in that way was able to hear and learn what was going on with her staff. Then she eased into the question of documentation, but with an entirely different question. After the appreciative check-in she asked, "How many incidents of inappropriate documentation did we prevent last week—and how did we do it?" Her team came to life as they shared stories and learned from each other. Within three months the numbers of "saves" were up while the numbers of errors dropped significantly.

 It is easy. Just try it. Start your next conversation or meeting by asking, "Let's all share a story of something that has gone well in our lives since we last talked." Watch what happens as you illuminate the best in your staff and colleagues.

Humor: The Other Vital Sign

Humor and wit have long been recognized as a way to bring out the best of people and relieve stress. According to the research of Professor Chris Robert and doctoral student Wan Yan, humor has a broad positive impact on people and the workplace. They have written, "The use of humor, and the ability to produce and make humor, is associated with intelligence and creativity, two things highly valued in workplaces. ... Humor has a meaningful impact on cohesiveness in the workplace and communication quality among workers. The ability to appreciate humor ... to laugh and make other people laugh actually, has physiological effects on the body that cause people to become more bonded."[1]

The people we interviewed shared stories of times when humor made a difficult situation seem less worrisome, when it helped turn a tense situation into a hopeful one, or when it just made work more fun. One person told us about a time when the mere sound of laughter from the boardroom had a pivotal effect on morale:

> I worked at a company that was being bought out, and we were all very nervous. During this time our CEO would go into meetings with the other company executives to make decisions about the future of the company and our jobs. From outside the boardroom door we could hear him laughing. Even though he had the weight of the entire business on his shoulders, he was able to laugh. People heard his laughter and sighed in relief. We felt it would all be okay.

Without knowing it, this CEO's ability to laugh in a tense situation brought a level of calm to people with whom he worked. When a person in charge or someone with authority exhibits humor, it holds special significance. People often gauge a situation by how leaders respond. Leadership reactions can escalate difficulties or diffuse them.

Appreciative Leadership uses humor to bring out the best of situations; and in doing so, it brings out the best of people.

The capacity to laugh at oneself encourages an open, comfortable environment in which ideas, information, and communication flow freely. When people laugh about the inevitable glitches, they have energy to move on to the really important issues. Mary organized a coffee reception for the vice president's wife. Many prominent community people were in attendance. When the guest of honor poured cream in her coffee, it curdled in the cup. She looked up at Mary, who was terribly embarrassed and said, "It's okay, dear. I don't need the calories." Everyone within hearing range laughed making Mary feel at ease.

A workplace filled with lighthearted interplay is more likely to foster camaraderie and collaboration—key factors for well-functioning teams. Team members who heartily embrace the motto "Work hard, play hard" told us that if they are going to spend long hours working together, they might as well have a little fun and enjoy each other's company in the process. "After all," they said, "we spend more time at work than we do with our families!" Alicia told us about how her department developed a reputation as a high-performing team and the "go-to" unit within the company. She said it was because of their collective sense of humor and willingness to play:

> We played games every day. I would write a category on the whiteboard, such as rock bands with a color in its name—like Deep Purple or Black Sabbath. People came from all over the building to play. When we played this game, everyone was equal, our department was approachable, and the entire company got to know us. As a consequence, they believed in the decisions we made and trusted that we would execute them effectively.

Positive and appropriate humor can be a very effective Appreciative Leadership practice for bringing out the best of people and situations. Indeed, nurses at Lovelace Health System placed humor at the top of the list of practices that gave them strength for the challenging work of caring for people who are ill. Recognizing how often a funny comment brought a smile to the face of an ill child or a hospitalized adult, they decided to conduct an Appreciative Inquiry into "Humor: The Other Vital Sign." They interviewed each other—nurses from all departments—and shared stories of times when humor lightened their mood and enabled them to deliver quality care to patients and their families. In the process of telling and listening to stories of humor at work, they were renewed and enlivened for the work they had to do.[2]

When using humor in the workplace, we suggest that you follow these Hawaiian rules: "No rain, no rainbows"; "Speak softly and wear a loud shirt"; and "Tell the truth—there is less to remember!"

Strengths Spotting: A Daily Practice of Illumination

Ever notice that some people easily know what others want, care about, and are capable of doing? They are able to listen to what others are saying, watch their expressions as they talk, and at the same time draw out strengths, hopes, and dreams. They are *strengths spotters*. Strengths spotting is a talent that can be learned.

> Lynne was talking to a young associate who surprised her with news that she was going to miss a deadline on a project. Some leaders would have turned this into an opportunity to criticize the young associate—but not Lynne.
>
> In the course of the conversations, Lynne told the young woman that she perceived her as very achievement oriented and knew that she would not miss a deadline unless something very significant was happening. The young woman agreed.

Then feeling safe, valued, and strong enough, she admitted that, yes, she was having personal problems that were getting in the way of her work. Lynne asked if she thought it was a short-term or long-term issue. The young woman said she very much hoped it was a short-term situation. Together they decided to wait two weeks before seeking other assistance with the project. The young woman left the conversation feeling heard, knowing that she was seen as capable and trusted, and deeply grateful to Lynne for caring about her as much as the project.

As Lynne demonstrated, strengths spotters are good listeners. They are willing and able to hear news that they wish they did not have to hear. They are able to hear positive potential through the haze of problems, dilemmas, issues, and troubles. Because they seek strengths in people and situations, they readily find them.

Here is a good way to begin strengths spotting. Ask someone to tell you about something that gives her a sense of pride. Listen to what she says, watch her expression as she talks, make note of the strengths you heard in the story, and then share what you heard—naming and acknowledging the person's strengths and successes. Here is an example. Notice how the conversation flows from story to strengths:

Barb: How was your weekend?

Gary: Great.

Barb: Really, what did you do this weekend that made it so great?

Gary: I fixed up my car.

Barb: What did you do?

Gary: I got car plaster and paint, and my friend and I repaired all the nicks and holes in my car. I even took the key out of the passenger's side and filled it in and painted it. I have an automatic lock and I didn't need it. New cars don't even have them. You should see how good it looks—just like a new car!

Barb: What gave you the idea to do this?

Gary: I had an estimate to have it done in a body shop, and then I saw the paint and car plaster for sale. I asked my friend, and he said he would help me, and my dad had some of the tools we needed. It just seemed easy. And it was so much cheaper.

Barb: I can't wait to see it. Sounds like you really had fun doing it and you did a great job!

Gary: Yeah.

Barb: You are very creative and good at identifying the resources that you need to do things. I also notice that you are clever at figuring out how to do things for the best price.

Gary: Yeah [with a big smile on his face].

Barb: And you trust your own abilities to do things well.

Gary: Yeah—and my friend was a lot of help. I've got to get to work now. Talk to you later.

Strengths spotting can occur in a casual conversation, as in the example above, or it can occur in a formal setting such as in an interview with a job candidate. By asking for and listening to stories and thereby illuminating strengths, you can easily identify what a person wants to do and is capable of doing. You can then consider if this person's strengths are a good fit for the available job.

Strengths spotting gives you the information that you need to assign work, align strengths, and build strong teams. It also enables you to give the gift of illumination to others. By seeing, hearing, and describing strengths, you validate people, give them self-confidence, and offer up new and better ways for them to see themselves. You lay the foundation for or reinforce a stronger and more capable self-identity. Appreciative

Leadership turns potential into positive power and points the way to sustainable high performance.

Strengths spotting may help people move on to other jobs that are more suited to their strengths. Early in her career Mary learned this lesson from a sales director at a major computer company. He called saying he could not meet in her office because he had lent his car to an employee for a job interview, and he asked Mary if she would mind driving to his office. When she arrived, she learned the full story. He had a brilliant young engineer working for him who really wanted out of sales. An engineering position opened up at a customer's site, and he immediately sent the young man and a strong letter of recommendation to interview for the position. His belief was that a happy employee elsewhere would be better than an unhappy employee on his team. Not only did he know that the young man's strengths were a much better fit at the customer's site than on his sales force but he also felt certain that this young man could one day become a valued customer.

This lesson was reinforced during the focus groups we conducted. Repeatedly people said that the best leaders they knew were ones who helped people match their skills, abilities, and strengths to jobs. Appreciative Leadership helps people put their strengths to work.

One of our warehouse managers was going to college for a degree in engineering. He was smart and people oriented. We decided to give him a "CALIPER PROFILE." The results were striking. According to the testing company, he had great potential to be a fabulous engineer. We encouraged him to finish his degree, which he did easily. When he graduated, he got a job at Lockheed Martin. Today he is on their executive team. Good leadership helps people find their strengths and determines where best to use them—even when it means they leave your organization.

A Word about Trust

When we describe individuals as "trustworthy," we may be portraying them as honest, dependable, constant—perhaps even honorable. But *trust*—the verb—is something we *do*, not just something we feel. A conscious act, it is more than a simple response to another person's behavior.

Trust, by our definition, is the *confidence in and acceptance of what is.* Regardless of the situation, we can always trust people to be exactly the way they are. Imagine this kind of trust as a practice. Compare it to the more prevalent practice of expecting people to be what we *want* them to be —and then being disappointed when they're not! In contrast, our definition of trust enables us to observe with detachment rather than judgment—to watch with eyes and heart wide open. This, in turn, helps us to consciously illuminate a person's basic goodness.

Writer and educator Jennifer Fox advocates this kind of trust between parents and children. Indeed, she suggests that it's one of the more powerful means we have of helping children discover, develop, and use their strengths (what we have described as strengths spotting). Fox asks parents to identify things the child likes to do: things the parent can *trust* their child to do, perhaps even despite what the parent might wish. Then she asks parents to identify the hidden strengths that the habits or preferences demonstrate, and wonder, where else might their child apply these strengths? [3]

Using this process as a guide, Joyce reflected on her teenage daughter. With some chagrin, she noted how Elena liked surfing the Internet, texting her friends, and shopping for clothes. But reflection changed her thinking about the patterns. Indeed, they suggested inclinations that she deeply valued: deep comfort with technology, curiosity, warmth, a desire and capacity to connect with people, a strong aesthetic sense, and an attraction to novelty. Feeling positive and affirming about her insights, she crafted a "love letter" to Elena, flooding her with appreciation for who she was. The exchange strengthened their bond; and it began a conversation that continued as Elena began searching for colleges.

This practice of trust yields equally positive results at work. When Art became HR director, he inherited three team members, one of whom seemed overly bureaucratic. Constantly referring to the rules, she alienated people who called for advice, training, or facilitation. Weeks of coaching went nowhere; she became increasingly defensive and rigid. Only when Art opened his eyes and trusted Glenna did things begin to shift. Realizing that her cautious adherence to policy was a misdirected strength, he began inquiring into her previous training and interests. Within a month, they mutually chose to transfer her into the payroll department, where her knowledge of human resources systems would be directed toward developing consistent, lawful systems that would support both the organization and the workforce. Within a year, she was promoted to become head of that department.

By trusting people to be who they are, we tend to our own serenity. But in doing so, we also cultivate an environment of openness and acceptance that paves the way for others to see themselves through fresh and affirmative eyes.

Appreciative Coaching to Bring out the Best in Others

THE BEST LEADERS HELP PEOPLE LEARN AND GROW.

Illumination is a daily practice of Appreciative Leadership, and it can be built into human resource processes such as recruiting, performance management, and especially coaching. People often seek out coaches when they feel they are not able to accomplish their goals, or they simply don't believe they can do what they have agreed to do. They have lost track of their capabilities and need a bold reminder of who they are and how they succeed. People also enter coaching to get help taking the next step in their life, figuring it out and planning to get there. In all cases, being reminded of strengths helps people discover what they want to do next and know they have the abilities to do it. Coaching is a powerfully illuminating process.

The purpose of appreciative coaching is to bring out the best of another person by discovering, articulating, and magnifying strengths, patterns of success, and generative potential. It is a three-step process, elaborated in Table 4-2. In many ways it is like strengths spotting, following a flow from story to strengths.

TABLE 4-2 THREE STEPS OF APPRECIATIVE COACHING
Step 1. *Collect Stories through Observations and Interviews*
Take time to observe the person you are coaching, to interview others who work with her, and to interview her directly. Be sure to take notes on what you see and hear. Collect multiple stories of success from early career to the present. Be sure to ask about the details of each situation and what she did to contribute to the success of the situation. When patterns of success begin to emerge, you know you have enough information and a sufficient number of stories.
Step 2. *Analyze Stories and Observations to Identify Patterns of Success*
Review all the stories you heard and the observations you made. Analyze this data with an eye to identifying patterns of success. How does this person get started on projects that succeed? What is her thought process as she begins and progresses toward a successful conclusion? Who else is involved in her successes, and how? What skills, abilities, talents, and strengths does she demonstrate repeatedly? What does she do when trouble arises? How does she deal with differences? How does she know when a project is complete? When she has succeeded? Prepare to share the patterns of success that you identified, and write down one or two provocative questions that the data bring to mind. Plan how you will support the person you are coaching as she reflects on the implications of your findings.

(*Continued*)

TABLE 4-2 *(Continued)*
Step 3. *Share Patterns of Success, Listen, and Affirm*
Make an appointment to share the patterns of success that you identified. Be sure to tell the person that you are coaching that you have identified her success patterns and want to share them. Provide assurance that there will be time for dialogue and reflection. Plan at least one hour for this session.

Conduct an appreciative coaching session: share the patterns of success that you identified; ask the provocative questions you created; and most importantly, listen, affirm, care, and validate. |

Appreciative coaching is a relational process in which the coach leads by shining the light on the person being coached. It requires the ability to put yourself on hold and to be in the service of the best of the person you are coaching. It requires the ability to see and share someone's implicit positive potential in a manner that enables them to see and appreciate it themselves.

The following tips can strengthen your appreciative coaching sessions:

- Begin by checking in with the person you are coaching. Ask, "How are you doing right now? Is there anything you would like to share with me before we begin?"

- Ask if the person you are coaching has a specific goal for the session. Ask, "What is your goal for our session? What are you hoping to take away from this coaching session?"

- Rephrase the takeaway to show that you heard it. Briefly let the person know that you will help him achieve his goal.

- Clarify the amount of time you have and how you will use it.

- Be sure to use "I language" when you share what you have learned. For example, "I experience you as ... ," or "Based on your stories, I think . ..."

- Frequently ask the person you are coaching if what you are saying makes sense or if he has any questions. Allow him to respond.
- Validate and affirm his comments.
- Close by asking him to summarize what he learned in the session.

Appreciative coaching takes time. When combined with daily practices of appreciative check-ins and strengths spotting, it is a valuable process for deep conversation and "performance evolution" on a regular basis.

The Benefits of Appreciative Coaching

As part of our consulting practice, we use appreciative coaching to support executives, leaders, and managers. Over the years, some have used it to chart their course for the "First 100 Days" in a new position. Others have used it to strengthen their own Appreciative Leadership capacities. And still others have engaged in appreciative coaching to redefine career goals and support personal transformation. In each case, the power of illumination has made a positive difference—for the leaders, their teams, and their organizations.

The many benefits of appreciative coaching, as they have been described to us, include:

- It helped me connect the dots of my strengths and my work in new ways.
- It showed me how to apply my strengths to the long-term goals I set.
- It gave me language for things I knew but never articulated about myself.
- I got powerful new words to describe myself and my strengths.
- It made me curious about other peoples' strengths.
- It gave me permission to feel and be as I am.
- It showed me how I process things, how I work at my best.
- I found words to communicate my leadership expectations to people.

- It really validated me and gave me confidence.
- I took more risks because I knew how I worked at my best.
- It shined a spotlight on me at my best.
- I saw the direct correlation between my strengths and the tasks ahead of me.
- I became a better team player.
- It helped me reframe a life issue in a way that I could succeed.
- It was liberating. It freed me to do things I had put off.

 Knowing that there are many reasons to engage in appreciative coaching, reflect now on how you might benefit from appreciative coaching. Would you like help discovering your strengths? Are you in a career or life transition? Do you want help enhancing your Appreciative Leadership capacities?

And think about how your team members might benefit from appreciative coaching? Is it time that you became their appreciative coach? When will you begin?

Linking Strengths to Business Results

As many of the benefits of coaching point out, there is a direct relationship between the illumination of strengths and business success. Appreciative leaders attend to the alignment of strengths among people and with the business plan, department goals, and the overall organizational vision. When Dr. Michelle Carter was asked to serve as interim vice president of marketing for a Fortune 500 company, she was tasked with one specific objective: to create a marketing plan for the business in Europe and Asia within 60 days but to do it in a way that would ensure full buy-in by the department directors. Believing that engaging the team in a way that brought the team members' best to the process would be key to success, she began with a process that had team members directly link their strengths to their department's performance. The results were positively powerful.

I began by inviting the 19 members of the marketing department to an introductory meeting. I handed out four- by six-inch cards and asked each person to write his or her job description on one side and to outline his or her strengths on the other. The purpose of this activity was to invite reflection about how the team members' strengths aligned with their responsibilities to the organization and ultimately with the marketing plan we were creating. I asked them to carry their cards with them and to observe when they experienced alignment, and to be prepared to share it, over the course of the next 60 days.

During this time, we met every Monday and Friday morning for 30 minutes, to work on the marketing plan. We began each meeting with an appreciative check-in, sharing stories of when our strengths and responsibilities were in alignment. We then surfaced and addressed marketing plan issues. The cards worked wonders. Those who needed it had time to reflect in advance and were ready to share at the start of the meetings. Others were able to speak on the spot about their experiences. Team members enjoyed making connections and pointing out how various people's strengths would be needed to accomplish what we were putting in the marketing plan.

At the end of 60 days, the marketing plan was submitted and approved. The team members celebrated by hosting an interoffice golf game in the hallways of their office. One year later, the bottom line indicated the positive results of including the whole system in creating the plan: there was a 35 percent increase in gross sales over the prior year.

Showing the connection between strengths and business results helps people understand how they fit into the big picture. Knowing that their strengths and abilities are integral to success inspires people to give their best and to work with others in ways that also bring out their best. By aligning people's strengths with each other and with the purpose and goals of your organization or community, you create a powerful energy for excellence.

Root Cause of Success: Illuminating the Positive Core

Every person, team, and organization has a unique pattern of strengths, capabilities, and potential waiting to be discovered, liberated, and used in positively powerful ways. In the practice of Appreciative Inquiry, we call this the *positive core*. It is a description of the specific causes of success. It is a profile of the person, the team, or the organization's strengths when it is performing at its best; this profile is the result of a *root-cause-of-success analysis*.

Root-cause analysis is a classic tool used in the total quality movement to facilitate a rigorous analysis of failures. We have found it to be equally powerful for conducting a rigorous analysis of successes—for creating an inventory of strengths embedded in a project, a team, or an organization when it is at its best. As Figure 4-2 shows, a "fishbone," or "Ishikawa," diagram is a great way to illustrate and illuminate the positive core of a team, group, or organization based on their root-cause-of-success analysis. Figure 4-2 is an example of one group's current capacities and strengths for positive change.

Not only does a root-cause-of-success analysis give you information about your team and your organization at its best; it also shines the light on daily acts of excellence that all too often go unrecognized. It gives credit to high performers and sets the expectation that everyone else should follow their lead. By illuminating the best of people,

FIGURE 4-2
ROOT-CAUSE ANALYSIS: AN INVENTORY OF STRENGTHS

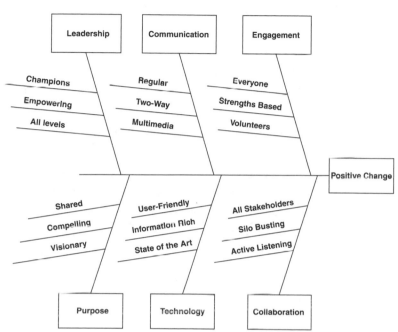

processes, and teams, Appreciative Leadership signals to others, "Do it this way and we will all benefit."

A major health care system invited a group of patients to talk about their local hospital at its best. The root-cause-of-success analysis clearly told its own story about what patients see as the best in health care: personalized attention along with standardized treatment, pain management, deep listening, access to information, and people who step out of their roles to provide compassionate care. They heard stories of the kitchen staff member who drew pictures and put them on food trays, the hospital housekeeper who ran a bath for a mother who had learned her son had cancer, and the physician who bought lobster and had the kitchen prepare a candlelit last dinner for a dying patient and his wife. The process opened their minds and their hearts.

Through the illumination of strengths, best practices, hopes, and dreams, people recognize untapped potential and learn how to become more positively powerful, personally and collectively. A root cause-of-success analysis is a valuable process for learning and strengths-based innovation.

All you need to lead the process is a group of people and two questions. First: "Tell me about a time when you experienced us at our best." Listen to the story, and probe to learn who, what, when, and how it happened. Second: "What caused us to be our best in this situation?" Analyze the story and repeatedly ask, "Why did it work so well?" and "How did we do it?" until you have fully illuminated all the strengths, capacities, and positive enablers in the story. Go around the group and ask everyone to share a story. After hearing the story, ask the whole group to analyze it. As you make the analysis, make notes on a fishbone chart like the one in Figure 4-2 or in any way that works for you and the group.

Take the case of Jim and his staff. Over a course of weeks, they explored their successes—times when they had performed at exceptional levels, in a variety of circumstances. Together, using a fishbone diagram, they conducted a rigorous analysis of their achievements. Just as Jim had learned from his total quality class, he asked how or why five times with respect to each and every skill, strength, or enabler cited in one of the staff member's stories. The conversation went like this:

Jim: Sally, your story illustrates terrific follow-through on the project you just described. How did you do that? [1]

Sally: By meeting one-on-one with all the team members, I helped them to follow through more effectively.

Jim: Why did you hold these one-on-one meetings? [2]

Sally: Because I knew it was crucial that I keep everyone informed.

Jim: Why? [3]

Sally: I'd gathered the team together early on, and we'd made agreements with one another regarding how we would ensure mutual accountability.

Jim: What made you decide to gather the team together up front? [4]

Sally: Well, on a previous team I'd discovered too late that it's important to know people's individual preferences and then to build them into the project assignments.

Jim: How? [5]

Sally: On that team, we had a big blow-up midway through implementation. Rather than tamping it down or waiting for it to blow over, I gathered people together so that we could talk through how we could restore the balance and finish the job with a greater sense of case and fellowship. A few people suggested that we ask everyone what he or she needed in order to stay focused and connected. It worked like a charm! Out of that blow-up, we established new agreements—and I saw the importance of starting with those kinds of agreements in the future.

Following this exchange, Jim, Sally, and the rest of the team members discussed and illuminated the strengths essential to their success. These included such things as meeting regularly; keeping people informed; being curious; being willing to learn from mistakes; honing great communication skills; acting with humility; and sustaining a deep belief in tapping into and drawing on each other's wisdom and capacities.

By engaging in a root-cause-of-success analysis such as this, leaders can illuminate people's strengths and build value for their teams and their organizations. Oh how readily, however, do some people describe the errors of another's way or why something is not as they believe it should and could be. When a customer receives bad service, she or he tells seven people. When a customer receives good service or even extraordinary service, she or he tells one, maybe two people. Why is this?

The answer lies in habits of communication. Most people have learned at home, at school, in the military, and at work that complaining gets attention, that finding and fixing problems gets rewarded, and that analyzing the root cause of failure builds knowledge to prevent future failures. All of this may be true.

What is also true is that complaining makes others feel blamed, causes fear, and creates an emotionally unsafe work environment. Being a problem fixer means that you need problems to succeed and to feel good about yourself so you become a problem spotter rather than a strengths spotter. It is also the case that a root-cause-of-failure analysis is a look-back over the past and often overlooks what is needed for innovation in the future.

These institutional habits are as hard or harder to change than personal habits. One way to change the "squeaky wheel gets the attention syndrome" is with a *root-cause-of-success analysis*. By inviting team members or a cross-functional group of people to identify and discuss what causes their success when they are at their best, you send a clear message that what you value and want to understand is success. Give it a try and notice the positive changes that occur.

 Take a moment now and think about when you might use a root-cause-of success analysis. Consider the following applications:

- To build an understanding among new team members about what makes a successful team
- To end a project on a good note by recalling what made it go well
- To learn what your customers appreciate about your service when it is at its best
- To engage people in dialogue and learning about leadership excellence.

Experiment with the process and make note of your results.

Creating a Positive Emotional Environment

BE PEOPLE CENTRIC. WHEN YOU GET TO KNOW THE PEOPLE YOU ARE LEADING, THINGS WILL FALL INTO PLACE AND THE RESULTS WILL COME.

From construction workers to office workers, from frontline employees to volunteers, from green-collar workers to executives, individuals want to be recognized for who they are and what they can do, as well as for what they achieve. Traditional leadership practices encourage recognition and appreciation for a job well done after the fact. Appreciative Leadership liberates positive power by recognizing people first; by making relationships; and getting to know people's needs, wants, hopes, and dreams along with their implicit capacities and strengths.

Recognition is an investment, not a reward. And it can have great payoffs, as the following story illustrates:

John ran one of the largest maintenance operations in Iraq. Four or five Turks were assigned by subcontractors to work for him. Initially, as soon as he had left the room, they would curl up and take naps. They weren't motivated. John's response was to take the time to learn about them, through which he discovered that they weren't getting breakfast, so he brought food for them. He learned who they were and where their families were from and what made them tick. He said that, in the end, they were actually eager to work for him. They called him "Baba," which means brother. They would come in every morning and say, "What more can we do? Tell us."

Professor of Positive Psychology Barbara Fredrickson determined, through her research, that humans flourish when they are in an environment of positive emotions.[4] She found that people who are surrounded by positive emotions such as hope, joy, optimism, love, confidence, trust, and happiness have a greater openness and broader capacity to learn and grow from new experiences. She calls this her "broaden-and-build theory of positive emotions." It makes sense. When we feel safe, we are open to new possibilities. On the other hand, she also found that when people are surrounded by negative emotions such as anger, fear, scarcity, criticism, and blame, their "fight-or-flight" tendencies go into gear and they become defensive and unable to listen, learn, or see new options for action.

More specifically Fredrickson's research shows that much of what leaders try to create in organizations today such as collaboration, achievement, and innovation requires positive emotions such as compassion, love, perseverance, and play at work. Our research folds directly into hers. The people we spoke with want leadership that cares about them, creates a safe environment for learning, and uses power to make a positive difference in the world. They want to live and work in a positive emotional environment.

The best way to ensure a positive emotional environment is to manage the ratio of positive to negative conversations in your organization. Members of successful teams,[5] organizations,[6] and even couples[7] talk three to five times more positively, hopefully, and appreciatively about their group and its members as they do negatively. The ratio of five positive conversations for every one negative conversation seems to be the determining factor for a positive emotional environment. Leaders who are critical, or who foster critique and problem solving as "the way of doing things," unintentionally tilt the emotional environment of their organization toward the negative. In doing do, they are stifling creativity and high performance. In contrast, leaders who put forth vocabularies of strengths, capabilities, hopes, and dreams, those who are generous with affirmation and illuminate the best in people and situations (even when they are not always at their best), create positive emotional environments that nurture innovation and high performance.

Since high-performing, positive emotional environments are created one conversation at a time, consider what you can do to change your conversations. Before reading the next chapter, take time to tell two or three people what you value, appreciate, and respect about them. You'll be glad you did.

Enhancing Your Capacity: Resources for Further Development

TABLE 4-3		
ILLUMINATION: A SUMMARY OF KEY PRACTICES		
	Key Practices	**Page Numbers**
Personal	• Positive self-talk	62
One-to-one	• Strengths spotting	67
	• Appreciative coaching	72
Team or group	• Appreciative check-ins	64
	• Root cause of success analysis	78
Whole organization or community	• Create a positive emotional environment	82

Recommended Books

Appreciative Intelligence: Seeing the Mighty Oak in the Acorn by Tojo Thatchenkery and Carol Metzker (San Francisco: Berrett-Koehler), 2006.

Authentic Happiness: Using the New Positive Psychology to Realize Your Potential for Lasting Fulfillment by Martin E. P. Seligman (New York: Free Press), 2002.

Now Discover Your Strengths by Marcus Buckingham and Donald O. Clifton (New York: Free Press), 2001.

Recommended Web Sites

Authentic Happiness

www.authentichappiness.sas.upenn.edu

This Web site, offered by Dr. Martin E. P. Seligman, director of the Positive Psychology Center at the University of Pennsylvania, has nearly 700,000 registered users from around the world who seek to learn more about the field of positive psychology and to gain insight into themselves and others.

Strengths Finder

www.strengthsfinder.com

Gallup introduced the first version of its StrengthsFinder online assessment in the management book *Now, Discover Your Strengths* in 2001. Since then, other books and the StrengthsFinder tool have helped millions to discover their top five talents.

VIA Institute of Character

http://www.viacharacter.org/

Approximately 1 million people worldwide have taken the VIA Survey online to find out their character strengths. VIA classification identifies 24 character strengths that have been found to be universal—characteristics that define what's best about people.

FIVE

The Genius of Inclusion: Engaging with People to Cocreate the Future

GEORGE'S STORY

Sponsored by the state's department of education, 150 people gathered for three days to determine the fate of their school for the deaf and the blind students. Despite the school's success, a rumor was circulating that the state legislature was planning to close it. The concern of parents, students, faculty, and staff—for the school and their own futures—had moved from worry to fear and anger. People had gathered to make a decision and offer recommendations for the future of services for students who are deaf and blind. It was an open public forum, and anyone who wanted to attend was welcome.

Participants included deaf students and adults, blind students and adults, parents, teachers, administrators, American Sign Language interpreters, Braille recorders, representatives from the governor's office, state legislators, and leaders and members of both deaf and blind advocacy groups, as well as interested citizens and guide dogs.

A turning point came on the first day, following appreciative interviews. Improbable pairs had shared their experiences with the school, its benefits to the community, and their hopes for its future. A woman stood and waved for the microphone. She introduced her interview partner, George, who was a local businessman, and herself, a state legislator. And then she said, "I arrived this morning certain that the school needed to be closed. Now, after hearing George's story, I am certain the school is a valued community resource that must be saved. I intend to support it fully." The room let out a collective sigh of relief.

What was George's story? George was sighted. His wife was blind. George's wife had attended the school where she received an education in life skills as well as academic subjects. She went on to become an outstanding teacher. And, as George told the story, she was able to marry him. All of that happened because of what she had learned as a young adult at the school for students who are deaf and blind.

The next day 150 people voted unanimously in favor of the school. One month later, the state legislators affirmed their decision.

Inclusion—consciously engaging with people to cocreate the future—is a foundational strategy for Appreciative Leadership, and an indispensable practice for unleashing the positive power of today's multicultural, multigenerational, and multitalented workforce. Realities are crafted in relationship, through conversations and collaborations. In order for decisions and plans for the future to satisfy and serve diverse groups of people, all the people whose future it is must be invited into relationship and included in the dialogue and decision making.

Imagine that you are planning an event to determine the future of a school. Who would you include on the invitation list? Faculty, administrators, parents, students, and who else? One school included cooks, janitors, board members, bus drivers, and graduates in their strategic planning process. Or imagine convening a meeting to consider alternatives for providing community health care. Who would you include? Yes, physicians, nurses, administrators, politicians, and patients are among the many voices that need to be invited and engaged. How about pharmaceutical companies, social workers, educators, laboratory technicians, and local media? In every situation there are many people, groups, and organizations with a stake in the outcome, all of whom can make a valuable contribution. All of whose voices matter, and all of whom will be enlivened through participation.

You get the idea. When we say *everyone whose future it is,* we mean all the relevant and interested people: everyone who has a stake in the outcome. We mean everyone who may, in some way large or small, be affected by the process, the decisions, or the resulting actions. Everyone whose future it is.

Your future may be a situation as simple as setting an agenda for a meeting next week or as complex as effecting change within a 10,000-person corporate culture. It might refer to the need to schedule vacation times, set sales targets, or strengthen union/management relations. Whatever the situation, conscious inclusion is essential for ensuring resources, fostering commitment, and successfully creating a future that works for all.

Some leaders choose not to be inclusive. They are content to work with a limited pool of potential. They repeatedly invite the same people, who think the same way—their way—to serve on teams and committees. They attempt to solve problems without engaging stakeholders, often for fear of revealing the organization's "dirty laundry." And they continuously tell people what to do, rather than inviting them into dialogue and collaborative decision making. As a result, they lose the many benefits of a high-engagement, inclusive work environment.

Appreciative Leadership, on the other hand, draws on the generative capacity of inclusion. By inviting diverse groups of people to coauthor their future in teams, departments, and whole organizations, you and your organization will benefit from the collective wisdom of collaboration. You will foster commitment to shared visions, goals, and paths forward. And you will evoke inspired action on behalf of the whole.

Inclusion Begins with You

Acts of inclusion range from the sublimely personal to the strategically global. Even, and especially, the healthiest of us carry multiple voices—some logical, some intuitive, some the voices of our parents and teachers, some the voices of experience. On this deeply personal level inclusion is about acknowledging, listening to, and making sense of your self-talk—your inner dialogue. The more you welcome, draw on, and develop the multiplicity of voices you yourself carry, the more likely you are to welcome and honor the voices of others.

Languages are among the greatest tools of Appreciative Leadership. To read, write, or speak a language is to understand the context, culture, and constraints of its people. Learning languages—be they Painting, Poetry, Music, English, Spanish, Arabic, Mathematics, Finance, or Marketing—enhances your capacity for Appreciative Leadership by enriching vocabularies, expanding ways of knowing, and opening you to new possibilities and paradoxes. The more inclusive and diverse your self-talk, the more inclusive and diverse your Appreciative Leadership practices can be.

Your range of inclusion is apparent in subtle and not so subtle ways, in your actions, your language, and your writing. On a break during a workshop, one of the participants asked to talk with us. She said we were not being inclusive in our facilitation style. We asked her to explain what she meant and to give us examples, which she did. We had a number of young people in the class, and it seemed to her that we were not affirming their ideas as frequently as we were the older, more experienced participants. We thanked her for her observation and said we would self-reflect as we went through the rest of the day. Sure enough, she was right. We were skipping over the comments of younger participants and consistently reinforcing the ideas of older participants. Our habits of facilitation were not in alignment with our value of full-voice participation. Having recognized this, we could do something about it. Indeed, we had to do something about it. As a result, we are now not only better able to demonstrate our value of inclusion but also more sensitive to when it is missing.

What voices, information, and ways of knowing do you consider valid, relevant, and useful? Whose ideas do you include and validate? What kind of information do you listen for as you make a decision?

People want leadership that is inclusive; that invites the ideas, thoughts, and feelings of diverse people; and that recognizes and affirms the good work of many different people. People are "turned off" by leadership that leaves them out of the story or makes them less important than others. Helen's "tale of two authors" makes this point clearly:

I received a copy of a highly acclaimed new book. The topic was of great interest to me, and the authors were respected authorities in the field. When it arrived, I made a cup of tea and settled in for an afternoon of reading. Within a short time I stopped reading and put the book down, never to pick it up again. In the first three chapters of the book, only the voices, experiences, and ideas of men were included. There were no citations or references to the work and ideas of noted women executives, professors, or practitioners. I could not believe it. The year was 2008. How could this be?

In contrast, a few days later I received another new book in the field. This book abundantly quoted, cited, and referred to the work of female as well as male colleagues. It contained photographs of women and people of color at work. It was an inclusive document. As a result, I found it easy to read, to refer to others, and to draw upon in my work.

The more broadly you allow yourself to think and feel, the more welcoming you will be to others' diverse thoughts and feelings. By expanding your capacity to seek out both sides of an issue or multiple perspectives in any situation, you expand your capacity for inclusion.

Casey recalled how he learned to be open and curious about different perspectives while in college:

> It was a policy class. We had to read articles describing all the different issues related to a specific policy. In each class we would read articles about a current event and discuss it. Then we would have to make up policies for each side of the issue. We would do this in small groups. We had to engage with each other, make a decision, come up with an example to show how our policy would work, and then explain why it had merit. This forced us to see both sides of the argument at the highest level. We couldn't come up with a good policy unless we understood the situation from all of the different perspectives.

Your inner dialogue—what you think, feel, and talk to yourself about—is informed by your life experiences. It, in turn, is the starting point for all that you say and do. It guides how you make relationships, and with whom. Your inner dialogue frames your practice of inclusion. It resonates outward and becomes apparent to others through your actions, language, and writing.

The practice of Appreciative Leadership holds all people in positive regard. Not some people, and not just people you agree with or who are like you, but all people.

 Take time now to reflect. How inclusive, open, and accepting of all people is your inner dialogue? When you talk to yourself about other people, are you accepting? Are you judging and blaming? Do you consider people problems to be solved? Or do you reflect and wonder about strengths and seeds of potential?

Issuing the Invitation:
Involving All Stakeholders

CONSIDER ALL CITIZENS AS YOUR CITIZENS.

At the level of interpersonal interaction and relationship with others, inclusion is about whom you invite into conversation. Every day you issue dozens of invitations—to those you say hello to in the morning, to those you hire, to those you invite to a meeting, to those you call on to speak in the meeting, to those you talk with at a party, to those with whom you do business. All of these invitations of inclusion say, "I value you and include you in my world. You are important. I care about what you think and feel and about what matters to you." Relationally, inclusion is an act of interpersonal validation and acknowledgment. Inclusion is a gesture of acceptance. By *issuing the invitation*, you begin the process of engaging people in coauthoring their future.

Appreciative Leadership practices are based on social constructionist theory and the notion that the creation of meaning occurs through collaborative activities.[1] Relationships, conversations, and social interactions are the sites of meaning making and world construction.[2] This suggests that who is included in a conversation matters. Meaning depends on inclusion. My meaning and your meaning, my department's meaning and your department's meaning, will be different until we talk with an intention to cocreate "our" meaning.

A conversation among executives, for example, sounds different from a conversation on the same subject among frontline employees. Two such conversations on the topic of cost containment occurred in an electronics manufacturing company. The conversation among executives ended with the questions, "Why are our employees wasteful? Why are they not cost conscious?" The conversation among frontline employees ended with, "Why won't the executives tell us what the materials cost? We know they want us to be more cost conscious, but how can we do that if they don't give us the information?" Meaning is made in conversation. Thus it was not until all levels of this organization met together, to discuss and determine a path forward for cost containment, that the two conversations came together. With everyone engaged in the same conversation, a shared vision and path forward—calling for action by everyone—was coauthored and carried out successfully.

As this story illustrates only when all levels, experiences, and ranges of diversity are in the conversation can you achieve full-voice engagement and commitment. Recognizing this, Appreciative Leadership hosts meetings and forums for diverse groups of people to come together to share ideas, interests, and concerns. Even when holding positions of authority, Appreciative Leadership leverages the positive power of inclusion and coauthorship. For example, the dean of the school of nursing's invitation list for a recent strategic planning summit included faculty, staff, and students, as well as community and hospital nurses, physicians, medical students, and patients. Everyone who had an interest in the future of the school was invited to attend and to participate fully in coauthoring its future together.

In ancient Greece, it was thought that all groups, communities, and gatherings have a *genius*: a spirit that animates their conversations, decisions, and activities. The *genius of inclusion* emerges when all relevant and interested people have a voice in the dialogue and decision making: when they are invited to coauthor their future together.

What people want from leadership has changed dramatically over the past decade. People no longer want leaders who are bosses, who act as if they know best. The people we talked with said that they are not moved to follow authoritarian, command-and-control leadership. Now, people want leadership to include and engage with them. They want leadership to facilitate collaboration. A successful architect described how this shift has changed the way he works:

The new and innovative Leadership in Energy and Environmental Design (LEED) process is based on inclusion. It requires that all the stakeholders involved in constructing a building get together to plan the building process. Architects, engineers, and subcontractors from all the trades collaborate right from the start. Historically this just wasn't done. It is a new process that avoids all the glitches and blame that come from lack of coordination. It makes things go a lot smoother, and it saves time and money, in the end.

Appreciative Leadership invites all the relevant and interested people and groups into the conversation. In contrast, authoritarian leaders are exclusive. They talk about people and make decisions for them. No matter how well intended, when this happens, when the future is socially constructed by some of the people, the rest of the people get restless. Exclusion fosters disengagement and lack of commitment to shared outcomes, collaboration, and quality. Appreciative Leadership asks, "Who needs to be involved to ensure success?" The genius of inclusion comes when you identify, invite, and engage with all the relevant and interested stakeholders for a given issue, project, or process.

Table 5-1 shows a list of categories of stakeholders for your consideration. It is designed to help you determine whom to invite to meetings and events. First, identify the groups, departments, and functions that need to be included. Second, identify specific people in each area. Use it when you want to expand the diversity of people you invite. It can be helpful when determing whom to invite to meetings, project planning sessions, team development programs, and community planning events, as well as strategic planning sessions. The table is a useful tool for determining and enhancing inclusion in any dialogue, decision-making, or planning process.

TABLE 5-1
CATEGORIES OF STAKEHOLDERS

Categories of Stakeholders	Group, Department, or Function	People
Information: People or groups who have knowledge or information needed to make decisions	• Practitioners	
	• Researchers	
	• Users	
Influence: People or groups whose position, knowledge, or resources give them influence in the decision-making process	• Executives	
	• Policy makers	
	• Board of directors	
Responsibility: People or groups who are responsible for carrying out the decisions	• Frontline staff	
	• Supervisors	
	• Managers	
Impact: People or groups whose relationships and activities will be impacted by decisions and outcomes	• Customers	
	• User groups	
	• Youth	
Investment: People or groups whose investment of time, money, research, people, space, materials, and so on is needed for success	• Suppliers	
	• Shareholders	
	• Foundations	
Interest: People or groups who have an interest, emotionally or relationally, in the outcomes	• Advocacy groups	
	• Family members	
Innovation: People or groups whose different ways of thinking and being and whose life experiences can bring novel ideas and ways of working to the process	• Think tanks	
	• Artists	
	• Futurists	
	• Youth	
	• Elders	

Reflect now on a time when you experienced the genius of inclusion firsthand. Someone may have involved you in conversation or decision that you both cared about and were affected by. Or you may have done the same for someone else—perhaps a remote or distant stakeholder. Whatever the situation, this purposeful act of inclusion yielded truly positive results. Recall the deteails.

Making It Safe to Speak Up

Issuing the invitation is the starting point for inclusion. For many, it represents a huge step forward, and yet it is not sufficient. Key to unlocking the positive power of inclusion is the capacity to make it safe for people to speak up. The more diverse your team, group, workforce, or community, the more conscious you must be about creating safe spaces and processes for communication, engagement, and full-voice participation.

Keep in mind that when you invite people to participate, they will expect to have a say. Do not make the mistake of issuing the invitation and then talking at people. When you ask people to share their ideas, to join a team, to participate in a meeting, or to be part of a process, be certain to listen to what they have to say. Take the time to design and facilitate participatory processes that give everyone an opportunity to speak and to be heard.

We find it useful to follow a *conversational progression* that starts the conversation with one-on-one appreciative interviews, or in a small group by going around the room and giving everyone a turn to talk. This establishes the expectation that everyone's voice will be heard and valued. From there you can comfortably move to small group discussions, and then to large group reports, dialogue, and decision making. This conversational progression works well for all types of gatherings from staff meetings to project review meetings to large-scale conferences and strategic planning meetings. An executive we coached learned to begin her presentations by forming small groups and asking people to generate questions for her. When right in the beginning she gave people an opportunity to share what mattered to them, they felt both included and ready to listen to what she had to say. Try using a conversational progression like the one we've described the next time you hold a meeting or give a speech. Invite others to talk before you speak, and see what happens.

The difference between a workplace where people feel safe to speak up and one where people are afraid is palpable. When people feel safe at work, they engage with each other in open conversations and collaboration about work, they share accounts of their personal lives with each other, and they spend time together, at work and in leisure. In a workplace where people do not feel welcome or safe to share their thoughts, opinions, or ideas, interactions are stiff and polite. Mark might even say, oppressed:

He became president of the largest and most profitable division of a multimillion-dollar consulting firm. With over 75 people in 20 countries reporting to him, the new job was immediately fun for him. Within a few weeks, however, he realized that not many others were having fun at work. There were few conversations about life outside of work, and fewer still about actual client work. The organization was tense and guilt ridden. People were coming to work late, walking into meetings that were already in progress, and disrupting work with constant apologies. There was no good time for collaboration.

Recognizing that he had inherited a less-than-positive work environment, Mark got curious about what it would take to change it. He gathered people to talk about what was going on. He invited everyone, from the best performers to the most troubled and troublesome professionals. Only after he reassured them that they were not in trouble, and would not be punished for being honest, did they began talking. As they talked, he listened. He quickly learned that there were a significant number of single parents and new parents on the team, all with a deep wish for flextime. Mark was stunned and questioned out loud, "In this day and age, how can this highly profitable, professional organization not have flextime?" It was true. And furthermore, when Mark suggested that the group design a flextime policy, he was told, "They won't accept it." "Who," asked Mark, "are *they*?"

Mark uncovered a deep practice of exclusion and oppression. Smart professionals were not included in discussions about performance and productivity. They had never been asked what they needed to be their best. He quickly turned that around. The discussions became a regular monthly event focused on: "What do we need to talk about to support our performance and productivity?" As people saw that they would not get in trouble for talking and that their ideas would be implemented, more and more people began joining in. Attendance grew to encompass everyone in the division, including whoever *they* were and Mark's boss the CEO.

As an appreciative leader, it's your job to set the expectation and make it safe for open and honest communication. When people realize they won't get into trouble by speaking up, they begin to talk. When they experience their ideas being listened to and validated, even if not acted on, they begin to share. When they see leadership's commitment to open and honest communication, they follow.

Leveling the Playing Field

There are status and authority dynamics present in every situation and every conversation. By virtue of their status, resources, presence, style, gender, race, or culture, some people are granted conversational privilege and become the focus of attention. Their ideas often carry more weight than those of others in the conversation. The presence of position and authority dynamics creates a particular need to actively ensure an equal voice for everyone.

Appreciative Leadership attends to equality of voice. It makes certain that everyone who wants to contribute feels safe and has an opportunity to do so. Appreciative leaders lead with questions and listen more than they talk. They may even stay out of the conversation altogether. This story shows how conversation opened up when a professor left the room, and the status and authority dynamics of his position were no longer present:

> I was taking a religious studies course. Though the professor kept trying to stimulate discussion, the students remained quiet, deferring to his ideas. One day he came into class and asked, "Is it possible to raise children in a home without the existence of God?" Then he walked out of the room. We all sat there just looking at each other, wondering if we were supposed to follow him. Then one student began to answer the question—and others followed. Soon we were all sharing ideas and answering the question in our own ways, talking about our own values and the moral and ethical issues related to religion and God. We shared a lot of personal experiences and made deep connections. It was one of the best classes I ever had, and he was one of the best professors I ever had. I still remember him today.

As this story illustrates, Appreciative Leadership is aware of how status and authority dynamics influence people's willingness to participate. Appreciative Leadership finds ways to share authority so that everyone feels invited and safe to openly communicate and participate in coauthoring the future.

Appreciative leaders balance the power of their position with the positive power of inclusion. They find creative ways to participate in conversations as equals. By leaving their titles at the door, they foster safety and confidence among those whose voices are not often heard. They sidestep attempts to make themselves the center of attention and authority by evoking self-organizing and shared responsibility. The leadership of the U.S. Navy, for example, circumvented the significant pressure of hierarchy in a series of three-day Appreciative Inquiry Summits. To achieve their purpose—*to cultivate leadership at all levels*—would require a level playing field. So they called for casual dress at the meetings. Decorated admirals, suddenly indistinguishable from first mates, worked side by side with hundreds of other participants. By leveling the playing field, the leadership unleashed unprecedented levels of grassroots engagement, insight, and collaborative action.

Innovation: The Business Case for Inclusion

Appreciative leaders practice inclusion for a number of reasons. It is the right thing to do to give people a voice in their own future. It ensures shared visions and collaboration. It builds trust, respect, and a positive emotional environment. The strongest case for inclusion, however, is that it is a key ingredient for innovation. Nothing stimulates creativity and innovation as well as inclusion. When the same people talk with each other about the same issues over and over again, the results are the same. When new people are invited into a conversation, new possibilities arise.

The leaders of Hunter Douglas Window Fashions Division engaged nearly 100 people—from frontline supervisors to the company's president—in their strategic planning process. Participants prepared in advance by reading reports of the business and conducting appreciative interviews focused on the company's competitive strengths and opportunities. During the meeting they articulated the division's core capabilities:

In the process a midlevel professional—someone who, in most organizations, would not have been invited to participate in strategic planning—articulated a business changing "ah-ha." As he looked at the information posted on flip charts around the room, he suddenly understood and communicated to others that the division's core capability had nothing to do with window fashions. Their core capability was actually the technology they used to create the window fashions. The room became silent. Everyone realized that what he said was indeed true.[3]

This crucial insight led the business to reinvent itself. A new strategic vision was crafted. Within a year, the company applied its core technology to the development of a new product in a new market: an acoustical ceiling tile. In this case, inclusion not only led to innovation but also to the formation of a new business unit and profitable growth for the company.

Many people learn about the importance of inclusion and its relationship to innovation the hard way: by failing to include people in discussions and decisions that impact their lives. By making the "error of exclusion" early in her career, one HR manager we interviewed learned that inclusion is the key to successful innovation:

My team was tasked to create a companywide employee development program. Initially, we created a series of programs and told employees about them. The programs were not successful. Attendance was low, and all the feedback told us that the programs were not relevant. We decided to try another route. We gathered groups of employees and asked them what they needed and wanted in the way of development. They gave us a lot of ideas. Some people even volunteered to help us create some of the programs. By including employees, we were able, finally, to create a unique, innovative, and highly successful companywide development program. And I learned how easy it is to be creative when you include other people. It was a good lesson to learn early in my career.

Innovation is triggered by the rich variety of ideas and information that are generated when you increase the diversity of your team or organization. New people bring new ideas. More people bring more ideas. Different people bring different ideas. The inclusion of new, more, and different people increases variety and stimulates innovation. We were asked by the leadership team of a pharmaceutical R&D laboratory to conduct an innovation assessment. Facing another year with no new discoveries, they began to wonder, "Do we have the right number and mix of scientists to stimulate innovation? Are we diverse enough? Do we have a scientific critical mass?" In talking with all of their scientists, it became clear that, no, they did not have enough variety among their scientists to stimulate innovation. They were too few and too specialized. They lacked the requisite diversity to spark the scientific imagination. As a result, they decided to reach out and form partnerships with the surrounding universities to enhance their scientific diversity.

If you want to increase the creativity and innovation in your work group or organization, draw on the positive power of inclusion. Invite a wide range of people and groups of people to join you in coauthoring the future.

Seeing through Beginners' Eyes

One group of people who can always be counted on to add variety and creativity to a conversation is youth. Be they chronologically young or simply new within a system, youth bring fresh ways of seeing and knowing, along with energy and a bias for action.

All too often the inclusion and participation of youth is a one-way street. They are invited to sit in, to listen, and to learn. When this happens, a valuable resource—the positive power of beginners' eyes—is lost. Appreciative Leadership welcomes youth and includes them as full participants. At an Appreciative Inquiry Summit on the future of their school, a group of students gathered to forge recommendations for the future. It was the first time they had been asked to offer their ideas. They were nervous. Their teenage voices wanted to operate an on-campus coffee shop. It would help them learn about business and entrepreneurship, and it would also provide a steady flow of their favorite beverages. It was their wisdom voices that prevailed. When asked to share their top-priority recommendation for the future, they said, "This is a great school. We believe it should seek out and welcome more diversity. We recommend scholarships to build diversity."

The capacity of youth to contribute positively and to awaken and draw out the best from others was discovered early in the development of Appreciative Inquiry. During an initiative called "Imagine Chicago," hundreds of people—old and young, teachers and students, business leaders and psychologists—conducted interviews to discover the strengths and lift up the civic imagination of their city. Professor David Cooperrider writes, "The very best interviews—resulting in the most inspiring stories, the most passion-filled data, and the most daring images of possibility—were conducted by *youth*."[4] Their openness, humility, and curiosity unleashed powerful conversations and untapped potential.

Youth participation and leadership offer the freshness of beginners' eyes along with positive expectations and commitment to a future that is theirs. People new to an organization or community also bring a fresh perspective. Whenever you have an opportunity to talk to newcomers, ask them to share who or what initially attracted them to the project, job, department, field of endeavor, organization, or community. Ask them to tell you about their initial excitement and positive expectations. Find out what they have learned since they began.

Think about the "youth" in your organization or community. Who are they? What special gifts do they have? How might you more fully engage with them?

The Wisdom of Elders

Another group to consciously include in conversations and decision making are elders—people whose years of experience add up to know-how, common sense, and wisdom. In many cultures the elders are respected community leaders. They are honored in a wide range of ways: by being listened to, by having their ideas considered, and by serving as mentors to youth. They are often the ones to bring perspective. Their life experiences give them the capacity to see and speak for the whole. They can often see where things are going, not because they have extrasensory perception but because they have been there before. Experienced members of any organization or community are valued resources. They are informational and inspirational sources of potential.

There are many ways you might elicit the perspectives and wisdom that elders can bring. The following are some ideas for you to try and see what happens:

- Create an elders' advisory council and call on the council to reflect upon and share ideas related to key issues and decisions.
- Establish a process for new employees to interview both older and long-term employees—to learn from them, to build relationships, and to foster cross-generational collaboration.
- Invite longtime staff members to participate on strategic teams or task forces.
- Ask elders to teach subjects of interest and experience to other members of the organization.

- Create a "Why you would want my job" campaign that enables elders to participate in recruiting new employees.

During an Appreciative Inquiry Summit, focused on the company's culture, Hunter Douglas Window Fashions Division set aside time for its elders—people with 10 or more years of service—to speak. They were invited to share stories from their past that illustrated the company at its best, that provided insight into unique strengths and skills, and that needed to be remembered going forward. The stories were rich and engaging—so much so that they were later assembled into a video presentation that was aired during new hire orientations. The film became an oral record of the company's history and strengths— an inspiration for future generations of employees.

Elders are the keepers of the stories. They are the ancestors on whose shoulders the future will stand. Recognizing the wisdom of elders, Appreciative Leadership actively includes those with seasoning, experience, and maturity.

Two Dimensions of Inclusion

Inclusion is two dimensional: wide and deep. *Widening* is the practice of extending the reach of your social network, to include more and different people in dialogue, decision making, and collaborative action. There are times when, in order to be effective, you need to widen your network of knowledge, perspective, and commitment— by finding ways to reach out and include more stakeholders.

This was the case for leaders in the city of Longmont, Colorado, as they began designing a long-range planning process. The community had a large and growing Latino population. The group leading the process was all Anglo. Recognizing the importance of engaging *all* segments of the community, the group invited Carmen—a well-respected, and highly skilled member of the Latino community—to join them. Because of her relationships, her cultural sensitivity, and her ability to adapt the process to meet the logistical needs of the city's Spanish-speaking citizens, Carmen's leadership yielded exceptional levels of Latino involvement in both planning and implementation.

As this case illustrates, work gets done through relationships. By reaching out and making new relationships, you enhance your pool of accessible ideas, information, strengths, and abilities. Just as important, you build commitment and establish the foundation for collaboration and productivity.

There are many creative ways to widen your reach of inclusion. For example, you might add new members to your team, host an Appreciative Inquiry (AI) Summit and invite all your stakeholders, host a series of webinars, put a blog on the Internet, form new partnerships, join and support professional associations, or volunteer to speak to high school or college graduates interested in your field.

Deepening, the second dimension of inclusion, is the practice of enhancing the quality and strength of relationships, whether they are old, new, or being renewed. All relationships need times of renewal. Work relationships are no exception. The need to care for and strengthen the quality of work relationships arises during times of transition, when trust has been broken, or when enhanced quality and service calls for improved collaboration.

Recognizing the need for better collaboration among the many people serving patients in the operating room, the director of surgery and the director of operations partnered to engage their respective staffs—physicians, nurses, radiologists, technologists, and administrators—in an Appreciative Inquiry process. People interviewed one another and shared stories of their best practices. They envisioned future collaboration and crafted a set of principles to guide their working relationships. During the process they got to know each other both as people and colleagues. As they got to know each other, admiration, respect, and trust increased. As relationships deepened, they began talking about and planning to standardize medical and administrative processes and procedures—with an eye on patient care. In this case, the deepening of relationships led to improved professional collaboration, which in turn led to enhanced patient service.

The many ways you can deepen existing relationships include team-building processes, face-to-face meetings, appreciative interviews, honest sharing of hopes and dreams, peer coaching, shared leadership of a project or event, volunteering together for a worthy cause, and spending social time together. Any practice that fosters sincere listening will foster compassion and mutual respect, strengthen the bond of trust, and deepen the quality of your relationships—at work and in your personal life.

Improbable Pairs

Creating venues for conversation among *improbable pairs* is a great way to foster and deepen relationships and build respect and trust among people at work. This notion comes from the process of Appreciative Inquiry. It refers to the practice of inviting people who don't know each other, or don't know each other well enough, to come together for an appreciative interview. It is a way of building bridges among people who see themselves as quite different and yet have some important reason for collaboration.

The practice is quite simple. First, ask members of your staff or team to choose a person in the group who is different from them. Tell them to select someone they don't know well, they don't work with regularly, and who is in some way very different from themselves. They may be different ages, genders, or cultures. They may work in different functions or have different educational backgrounds or areas of authority. Let them choose a partner based on whatever they believe are the greatest areas of difference. Second, give them a list of three to four appreciative questions, and tell them to take 20 to 30 minutes each interviewing one another. Third, following the interviews, ask them to share comments about their experiences in the interview process. The results will astound you as they have us. Time and time again when we ask people to partner up in improbable pairs, they discover and report on how much they have in common.

Positive dialogue among improbable pairs heightens people's appreciation for one another and builds a shared sense of identity. The practice of partnering in improbable pairs creates an opportunity for people to share their stories and be heard by another person—their partner. When this happens, everyone feels affirmed and valued. In return, they affirm and value their partner and what they have in common. This in turn, nurtures their relationship and sets the stage for future collaboration. Such an improbable pair bonded during a strategic planning meeting in a northern Colorado community, where a retired Japanese-American businessman and a 15-year-old Hispanic girl chose each other as interview partners because they looked so different from one another: he in a smart dark suit, and she in faded denim, stylishly torn in the teenage fashion of day. As they spoke of their vision for the city that brought them together, he told her about his life growing up in Japan, moving to the United States and building his business. She talked of her family, love of learning, and her dream to go to college one day.

Despite their differences, they forged a meaningful connection over the course of their 40-minute conversation. When the meeting ended, they stayed in touch. A few years later, with the permission of her family, the businessman sponsored the young woman's college education, citing it as one of the best investments he had ever made.

We have come to call this the *paradox of improbable pairs*. When we meet and sincerely seek to know another person who is different from us, we discover that we have much in common. Sincere inclusion builds trust, fosters respect, and enables us to recognize that we are all related in deep and meaningful ways.

Reaching out to the "Other"

Acts of inclusion can build bridges and heal relationships—at work, in families, and in society. When you reach out to people, you consider to be on "the other side"—your opponents, your competition, or even your oppressors—you create a pathway for reconciliation. Appreciative Leadership is dedicated to a world that works for all. It practices reaching out to the "Other" with deep listening, compassion, apologies and forgiveness, and a sincere willingness to go forward together. It takes courage to reach out and help others feel welcomed and valued.

Diana showed such courage a few years ago. As an honored guest in India, she was invited to give a speech at a large private school in New Delhi. Everyone in the school was invited to attend her presentation on Appreciative Inquiry. There were students, faculty, administrators, parents, and school staff in the room. Many were seated; some were standing in the back of the room. Knowing that people of different castes still do not interact easily with one another in India, she took a deep breath and invited those standing to find a comfortable seat. She pointed to empty seats at the tables in the front of the room. Fortunately, the values of the school, its students, and their parents were in alignment. They looked around and with open arms waved to those standing to come and sit with them.

Each and every one of us has an Other: a person or group of people whom we neither like nor trust—whose values or lifestyle choices we find disagreeable. We may even go so far as to attribute that which we find undesirable in the world to them. At work, people blame the Others for things that go wrong. In society people avoid them or speak out against them. Some people have little or no direct experience with their Others, and yet they see them as unworthy or inadequate. Their prejudice is deeply institutionalized.

Some people, however, do know their Others, having had a negative or even traumatic experience with them at some time in their past. Such was the case when citizens in postapartheid South Africa gathered to create a new future. An Afrikaner police officer partnered in dialogue with a black woman who had been both abused and imprisoned by the police. As the woman shared her story, her partner became visibly agitated—then began to cry. He acknowledged that he had carried out the same kinds of actions that had so harmed her. He asked for forgiveness—which she gave. In the end, they chose to work together on a project to rebuild their city and to offer others the same kind of healing experience that they had shared.

Such was the case when groups of Palestinian and Israeli women—all of whom had lost children in the conflict—came together to forge relationships and work for peace. They began by sharing their stories, by exploring their respective faith traditions' teachings about peace, and by sharing food. They laughed and cried, and together they envisioned the world in which they wished to live. They discovered what united, rather than divided them. And in the process each of them changed.

As is often the case, many people know the Other more through the stories they have heard about them than through actual interactions. By reaching out to the Others and getting to know them as people, you create new stories and forge new and positive impressions that can change you—and them—forever.

 Consider these questions. Who are *your* Others? How did you learn to see them this way? What have you lost by excluding them from your life? How might you reach out and include them, going forward?

Improbable Participation: A Risk Worth Taking

Taking the idea of improbable pairs further, appreciative leaders practice *improbable participation*. They invite people whose differences might otherwise cause them to be excluded into meetings, projects, and developmental programs. To do so is often a risk—one that inevitably pays off in rich rewards.

In one of our focus groups, we heard the story of a small town's chamber of commerce that took a risk of improbable participation, that paid off.

The list of applicants for the community leadership program included a young outspoken lesbian. She was a recognized informal leader with a very abrasive style. Her application created controversy and concern among the members of the selection committee. It would be a risk to include her in the class of 40 leaders. It would also be a risk not to include her. Ultimately, they decided to invite her to participate.

At the start of the program, the tension in the group was apparent. But over time, classmates began to bond, to feel safe, and to be open with each other. They told the young lesbian about what they called her "in-your-face" leadership style. This along with sincere appreciation for her positive contributions created a dramatic change. She was accepted by people that she appreciated and who appreciated her. She began to blossom. Gradually, her abrasive style disappeared. She became an effective community leader. A few years later she accepted an invitation from the local chamber of commerce to serve on its board of directors—a position that neither she nor members of the selection committee could have imagined four years earlier.

Improbable participation is a two-way street. It invites you to take a risk and include someone with untapped potential onto your team or into your meeting. It also invites you to be an improbable participant by joining a group, a network, or a meeting where you are the unlikely participant. It takes courage to be an improbable participant. Ask a colleague in a different department if you can attend her staff meeting. Go and learn. Take a class on a subject that interests you but is very different from your field of work. Attend another faith's religious service or celebration. Read their sacred text and learn. Study and become proficient in another language. Attend a meeting in your community on a topic with which you are not familiar, and seek to understand why it is important to the community's well-being.

Just as there are many ways to be an improbable participant, there are also many benefits. It is a great way to learn and make new relationships. Most significantly, however, by participating in meetings, events, or classes where you are the minority—the one who is different in age, gender, race, religion, ability, or culture—you will experience and may come to understand inclusion from the other side of the street. It will strengthen your Appreciative Leadership capacity to unleash the positive power of inclusion.

From Me to We: The Feeling of Belonging

One of the greatest skills of Appreciative Leadership is the capacity to create a sense of "we" among a diverse group of people. Robert, now a very successful public service executive, told us the story of Neil, a leader who was especially good at including newcomers and creating a sense of we. His story illustrates the important difference between being on a team and feeling like "we are a team."

In my early career as an aspiring manager, I worked for a series of supervisors who regularly pointed out my mistakes and reminded me of my responsibility to take corrective action. As a member of their team, I was expected to solve problems as they occurred, report results, and await the assignment of new problems. These teams did not operate as or feel like teams.

Later in my career I had the good fortune to meet Neil and be invited to work with him. When he became my supervisor, one of the first things he did was assign a colleague to work alongside of me. My peer mentor was there to answer my questions and to help me learn whatever I needed to know to succeed in my new job. His advice was always valuable to me because it was often based on the questions I asked—what

I needed to know at the time. I soon learned that I was not a "newbie" in the department but a full member of Neil's team. I was included in all meetings where we sat in a circle and took turns leading the meeting. Because of my past experiences, it took me a couple of months to realize that we were a team whose members supported each other in accomplishing the overall work. That is how I learned the difference between being on a team and feeling like we are a team.

Just as Neil included Robert as a full member of the team, appreciative leadership expects and encourages individuals to support and to contribute to the goals, plans, and intentions of the whole. They create situations and processes for people to support one another. They regularly bring the whole group together to deepen relatedness and to discuss and determine how to achieve their shared goals. Whatever the form of inclusion, when it is successful, people feel that they belong, that they and their contributions are valued, and that there is a sense of "we" working together for the good of the whole.

Accommodating Conversational Differences

To truly invite people to coauthor their future requires that you create opportunities for people—all stakeholders—to talk and to be heard. We have all been in situations in which a few people—the vocal minority—dominate the conversation. They use more of their share of talk time, and they are seemingly unaware of others' need to speak. Why does this happen? There are endless explanations; but we find it useful to understand three considerations that are frequently at play.

Extraversion and Introversion

A first factor at play in many conversations is the difference in the conversational style between extraverts and introverts. *Extraverts*

often think out loud—an act that helps them recognize what's important to them and make decisions. When asked their opinion about a
situation, they may offer a quick, unstudied reply. *Introverts*, on the
other hand, often prefer to reflect before talking. As a result, they may
not be as quick to respond, or they may wait to be asked before they
share their ideas. These are conversational preferences that appreciative leaders consider and balance in order to unleash the full potential
of a group.

To ensure that everyone—introverts and extraverts alike—gets a
turn to talk, we suggest you facilitate *taking turns talking*. It is a conversational discipline that takes practice and patience. Here is how
you do it. You raise an issue, a topic, or a decision for consideration.
Then tell people that you want to hear everyone's thoughts and feelings on the subject so you are going to practice *taking turns talking*.
Everyone must say something when it is his or her turn, even if it is
simply, "Pass." No one speaks a second time until everyone has spoken once. The practice is generally appreciated by three fourths of the
people in the room. The others may feel that it slows things down—
until they truly begin to listen. And then they too will experience the
benefit of taking turns talking.

A tool that can be used to encourage people to take turns talking is a *talking stick*—a ceremonial object used for centuries by Native
Americans "as a means of just and impartial hearing."[5] When important matters are being discussed, a talking stick is used to signal whose
turn it is to talk. It is passed from one person to the next, endowing
the holder with the right to speak and be heard. We have used talking sticks in a wide range of group settings from government leaders
to women religious leaders to executives to nurses. In each case, the
participants found the talking stick to be a valuable tool for positively
including everyone in important and even contentious conversations.

Right- or Left-Brain Dominance

A second significant difference in conversational and work styles
can be attributed to right- or left-brain preferences, also known as
hemispheric dominance. The left side of the brain, which is the seat

of language, processes things linearly and sequentially. The right side of the brain, by contrast, tends to be visual; it processes information intuitively, holistically, and randomly. For example, action planning and timeline scheduling are largely left-brain activities, while design and play are largely right-brain activities. Both hemispheres of the brain are involved in most human activities, and all healthy people regularly use both sides of their brains. Still, most of us have a preferred or dominant brain hemisphere, just as we have a dominant hand for writing.

To fully include and engage everyone, Appreciative Leadership regularly employs a combination of left- and right–brain activities to stimulate whole-brain thinking. Hunter Douglas Window Fashions Division did just this during one of its strategic planning summits. Participants crafted a written vision statement (primarily left brain) and then enacted it through song, art, and skits (primarily right brain). The combination of activities fueled people's imaginations and fostered business-related innovation. One group's playful drawing of a "virtual window covering" that would let people see whatever they wanted to see—a sunrise or sunset, the mountains or the ocean—stimulated another group to actively suggest the development of a "smart" window covering that would automatically respond to changes in light, heat, and time of day. Just as one person's play is another person's mental fertilizer, so the integration of right and left brain hemispheric activities stimulates creativity and innovation.

Many Languages

A third factor at play in many situations has to do with the many languages people speak. No matter what the language of your business, it is very common today to work with people whose first language is different from your own. In today's global work environment, this is true for employees as well as customers. For ease of conversation, this may require that you translate materials into multiple languages, that you provide interpreters, or that you conduct business in multiple languages.

A few years ago, while working with a Native American hotel and casino in New Mexico, we were surprisingly challenged by the diversity of the workforce. We had designed and were facilitating a series of five Appreciative Inquiry Summits focused on "Excellence in Customer Service." All 1,200 employees were invited to attend one of the two-day-long meetings. Wanting to be inclusive and welcoming of all, we planned to accommodate English- and Spanish-speaking employees by translating materials into Spanish and ensuring that our team included a Spanish-speaking facilitator. We did not plan, however, for the Chinese chef and his team of cooks and kitchen staff whose primary language was Chinese. They arrived at the first meeting ready to participate fully. We were the ones who were not ready. We apologized for our inappropriate cultural oversight. We asked them to wait and attend the next meeting, one week later. They agreed.

We quickly contacted a Chinese colleague who joined our team to interpret for them. Their participation brought great excitement and energy to the meeting. During report-outs in the whole group, the translator interpreted and presented their ideas in English, and then, at the request of the whole group, the Chinese participants shared their ideas in Chinese. Spanish speakers did the same. The result was a culturally rich environment in which everyone felt safe to share their ideas, thoughts and feelings, and to collaborate in creating the future of their workplace.

Wherever you are and whatever your goals today, it is important that you find ways to include others, to accommodate conversational differences, and to listen deeply. In so doing, you will stimulate innovation and support the creation of a world that works for all.

Taking Inclusion to Scale: The Appreciative Inquiry Summit

In today's rapidly changing global environment, the capacity for accelerated positive change is a key success factor. This means that organizations must be able to take inclusion to scale: to engage hundreds or thousands of diverse people in conversations about the future—their shared future—and get results. The Appreciative Inquiry Summit methodology is a powerful way to lead large-scale positive change, to rapidly and fully engage people in coauthoring the future they most desire, and to accelerate innovation through radical inclusion.

An AI Summit is typically a two- to four-day process that brings all of an organization's or community's stakeholders together to (1) discover their collective core competencies and strengths; (2) envision opportunities for positive change; (3) design the desired changes into the organization's or community's systems, structures, strategies, and culture; and (4) implement and sustain the changes.[7] AI Summits have been used by global corporations, nonprofit organizations, government agencies, health care institutions, and religious organizations including Hewlett-Packard, the United Way, the Environmental Protection Agency, the University of Virginia Health System, and the Sisters of the Good Shepherd.

By including everyone who has a stake in the future in one simultaneous conversation, unprecedented collaborative action is unleashed. In the words of Philip A. Gray, former general manager and vice president of McDonald's Central Division, "The Appreciative Inquiry Summit engages the 'whole system,' builds relationships, gets everybody on the same page, and produces results."[6] It is a powerful vehicle for taking inclusion to scale.

Enhancing Your Capacity:
Resources for Further Development

TABLE 5-2 INCLUSION: A SUMMARY OF KEY PRACTICES		
	Key Practices	**Page Numbers**
Personal	• Expand your inner dialogue.	92
	• Level the playing field.	99
One-to-one	• Issue the invitation.	93
	• Connect improbable pairs.	108
Team or group	• Invite improbable participation.	111
	• Accommodate Conversational Differences	114
Whole organization or community	• The Appreciative Inquiry Summit.	117

Recommended Books

The Appreciative Inquiry Summit by James D. Ludema, Diana Whitney, Bernard. J. Mohr, and Thomas. J. Griffin (San Francisco: Berrett-Koehler), 2003.

The Inclusion Breakthrough: Unleashing the Real Power of Diversity by Frederick A. Miller and Judith H. Katz (San Francisco: Berrett-Koehler), 2002.

The Power of Collective Wisdom and the Trap of Collective Folly by Alan Briskin, Sheryl Erickson, Tom Callanan, and John Ott (San Francisco: Berrett-Koehler), 2009.

Social Construction: An Invitation to the Dialogue by Kenneth J. Gergen and Mary Gergen (Chagrin Falls, OH: Taos Institute Publications), 2004.

You Don't Have to Do It Alone by Richard H. Axelrod (San Francisco: Berrett-Koehler), 2004.

Recommended Web Sites

Collective Wisdom Initiative

www.collectivewisdominitiative.org

This Web site was created in 2002 by the Collective Wisdom Initiative with the support of the Fetzer Institute to further the emerging field of collective wisdom, its study and practice.

The Taos Institute

www.taosinstitute.net

The Taos Institute is a nonprofit organization committed to exploring, developing, and disseminating ideas and practices that promote creative, appreciative, and collaborative processes in families, communities, and organizations around the world.

United Religions Initiative

www.uri.org

The United Religions Initiative (URI) was founded in 2000 by a global community committed to promoting enduring, daily interfaith cooperation and ending religiously motivated violence. Members from diverse backgrounds pioneer interfaith dialogue and peace-building skills. Its core organizational principles include inclusive membership, self-organizing initiatives, and decentralized governance.

SIX

The Courage of Inspiration: Awakening the Creative Spirit

A VISION BEYOND OURSELVES

With less than 10 years in ministry, Michael was an unlikely candidate for president of the church's national association. His opponent was widely known and well respected, with endorsements from many incumbent national leaders. Even with his strong track record of local success, Michael was the underdog.

His local congregation added over 400 new members at a time when churches and whole denominations were languishing. A stunning success by any measure, the growth was of particular note because it was in a community whose spiritual diversity was highly pronounced. A few years into Michael's tenure, a member of the congregation commented, "After 20 years of on-again, off again involvement, I am an enthusiastic, contributing member of this community.

Michael is a good leader. He gets excited about new ideas—even when they are not his own, and even if they don't jive with his worldview. He welcomes people and helps them bring their dreams to life."

And Michael had a dream, a vision of *"a religion for our time"* that called him so strongly that he invested tens of thousands of dollars and a year of his life to answer the call and campaign for office. "There are countless unchurched people who are seeking a spiritual home," he said. "They are the spiritually hungry that our denomination—with its liberal doctrine and inclusive practices—is uniquely suited to feed. *We can only fulfill this vision by radically reaching beyond ourselves* in ways we have not done in the past, by changing how we relate to each other and the world."

As he traveled from church to church, Michael's positive, hopeful message and path forward attracted many people. His campaign ignited their creative spirit and mobilized broad-based support around the country. In the end, his victory was decisive: a clear and compelling mandate for the denomination's future, and a testimony to the power of inspiration.

Inspiration abounds with a courageous invitation to transcend the status quo. It breathes life into new possibilities, offering hope in the midst of crisis, giving people a reason, and a way to go forward. It prompts innovation and actions not previously thought to be possible. Appreciative Leadership draws on this positive power of inspiration by fostering inquiry and dialogue about hopes, dreams, and visions. It unleashes otherwise latent potential—great ideas, strengths, capabilities, and skills—by inspiring creativity, confidence, and hope for the future. Even when all the necessary resources are available, nothing changes and nothing of merit happens without inspiration. Inspiration opens people to the source of life that moves through and among us all. It gives people hope and courage to shed habitual ways of living and working and move in new, innovative and more life-affirming directions. Inspiration, hope, and creativity—three essential ingredients for personal and collective transformation—go hand in hand.

Inspiration moves people to action. It gives them something to work for and toward in service of a better world. It calls forth their contribution to the whole. It encourages people to learn and to do what it takes to realize their dreams, achieve their goals, and help others do the same. Inspiration sparks the fire of excellence. It is the source of all achievement.

 Reflect for a moment: Think about a time when you were inspired; a time when you were moved to creative action. Who or what inspires you? What awakened your creativity? What gave you confidence to take action? What did you do?

We are all inspired differently. Seeing a leader speak from the heart, hearing another person's story of success, sharing a vision for a better world, seeing someone overcome an obstacle, witnessing an exemplary act of service, experiencing mastery, beauty, or joy. Whatever its form, inspiration creates a positive pull, a creative force that draws us toward a better life, a better relationship, or a better way of working.

Appreciative Leadership pays attention to what inspires people. During our research we heard story after story of leaders, coaches, and managers who were respected because they were attentive in this way. Whether their team was made up of 5 or 50 people, they watched and listened, and they learned what people cared about and what moved them to action. They learned what inspired the people with whom they work.

Do you know what inspires the people around you? It's easy to find out. Just ask them: "Tell me about a time when you were at your best. What inspired you?" Or watch them: when people feel inspired, they show excitement, enthusiasm, and high energy. Or listen to them; when people say things like "I don't know where this idea comes from, but what if we …" or "I have a creative idea that I need your help thinking through …" or "I would love to …," they are expressing their creative spirit. Some of the clues that tell you when people are inspired include joy, enthusiasm, energy, intuition, and creativity. An inspired workplace hums with the sounds of creative collaboration, synergy, and the surprise of collective wisdom unfolding.

Grounded in the Realities of the World

Inspiration, like a tree of life, grows with two large branches forking outward. One branch reaches out, drawing people in and attracting them to the good, the true, and the beautiful. It is the positive power of inspiration that stems from appreciation, beauty, awe, grace, love, and wonder.

The other branch reaches out over the hardships and distress of the world and gives hope. It is the positive power of inspiration that grows from compassion, deep belief in a better way, personal calling, and dedicated service to society. It is a loving determination to collaborate with others to do whatever it takes to change things for the better—one life at a time, one day at a time, one world at a time.

Both branches grow out of and draw us into the deep well of life-affirming energy that pervades everything. They awaken us, connect us, and help us become vessels of creation. They enable us to do our part in the cocreation of a world that works for all.

Appreciative Leadership holds a unique view. Looking out from the fork in this tree of life, it enables us to see the goodness, beauty, and excellence in the world, along with the distress, pain, and injustice. This unique perspective gives power to the inspirational practices of Appreciative Leadership. They are not naïve. Appreciative leaders are grounded in the realities of the world. It is their compassion and dedication that sends them seeking best practices and exemplary scenarios to adopt, adapt, and disseminate. Their belief—indeed, their insistence that things can and must be better—gives them courage and credibility to join with and inspire others:

An accomplished professor at the Seoul National University College of Medicine, Shin introduced himself to us at the start of the Appreciative Inquiry workshop as having "a little bit of organization development experience." He was curious and dedicated to understand this resolutely affirmative and relational approach to change.

It was only later, when he shared further, that we understood what inspired him. As a young graduate student in the late 1970s, Shin was involved in democratic protests against the government. The experience—and his belief in something better for his country—moved him to work as an organizer in the democratic resistance. For 14 years he coordinated, recruited, planned, and mediated, bringing together people of different backgrounds and beliefs around the compelling goal of a democratic government.

So what led him now to want to learn Appreciative Inquiry? "Ours is the only country that is still divided by political ideology," he said to the group. "It can't last forever. Some day, North and South Korea will reunify. And when that happens, we will need people with skills—more skills than any of us have today. We'll need to come together as one: to listen to one another, and to see beyond our differences. I need to be ready for that time. I need to learn *now* how to help."

Grounded in the realities of the world, Appreciative Leadership awakens the creative spirit, giving hope and moving people to collaborative action in service of a better way. Acts of inspiration can be large or small, global or local; they are all important. People with whom we talked said they are inspired daily by watching parents lovingly care for young children, by executives who "walk their talk" and show appreciation, by colleagues who say please and thank you on the job, and by people who smile and say hello as they pass you on the street—all small acts of kindness that open people's hearts and inspire resonant actions.

Crossing over to the Positive: It's Your Choice

Appreciative Leadership is a choice—to live and work in the energetically positive.[1] Seeing, experiencing, and knowing the hardships of the world, Appreciative Leadership chooses to be a life-affirming force for good, to discover and apply strengths and best practices, to facilitate collective wisdom defining a better way, and to inspire hope for the future.

Crossing over to the positive is a choice you make about how you apply and use your strengths. Consider a knife and ask yourself, "Is it positive or negative?" The answer lies not in the implicit nature of the knife but rather in the way it is used. If it is used to harm another person, its effect is negative. If it is used to slice and dice vegetables and herbs and to prepare a healthy and delicious meal, its effects are positive.[2] So it is with human potential. Appreciative leaders choose to apply both their own and others' human potential in support of life, to create better ways of living and working.

The choice to live and work in the positive influences what you choose to see and nurture in yourself and others. The folk tale of "Two Wolves" illustrates this lesson:

> One evening an old Cherokee man told his grandson about a battle that goes on inside people. He said, "My son, there is a battle between two wolves inside us all. One is bad. It is anger, envy, jealousy, sorrow, regret, greed, arrogance, self-pity, guilt, resentment, inferiority, lies, false pride, and

superiority. The other is good. It is joy, peace, love, hope, serenity, humility, kindness, benevolence, empathy, generosity, truth, compassion, and faith."

The grandson listened and thought for a while. Then he asked his grandfather, "Which wolf wins the battle?"

The grandfather smiled and replied, "The one you feed."

Appreciative Leadership inspires people by feeding the positive. Being positive creates a safe space for people to learn and grow. It gives people confidence that a brighter future is on the horizon, even when they are not doing well. People in our focus groups repeatedly told us that they are inspired by positive people and that negative people create fear and tension at work. They said that they enjoy being around positive people and that positive people inspire them to succeed. The dean of a prominent business school shared this story about his parents:

My first experience of positive power came from my mother. She always believed I would be successful. Even when I was not doing well in my classes, she would say it didn't matter. "You are going to be something big. Either you are going to be a doctor, or you are going to leave India and go to the United States." My dad, on the other hand, would say, "You are going to be a good for nothing. If you don't do better in school, you are going to be selling tickets at the theater." My father drove me with fear, but my mother drove me with love. Without the positive power from my mother, I would not be sitting here today. I listened to her instead of my dad because of the clear evidence of authenticity and love. She didn't just say I would be great. She showed it in many ways. I didn't want to disappoint her. When I came to the United States, I had only $250; so it was not as if I had the resources to easily make this happen. Her belief in me made me drive toward success.

It takes courage to choose the positive as a daily leadership practice—especially in the face of poor performance. We know that it is hard to let go of the tendency to criticize and instead be positive, caring, and supportive. And we know the results are worth it. A director of sales put it this way:

Over the years I have learned that if people perform poorly and I criticize them, I will get a defensive response and there will be no improvement in performance. If I instead approach them with care, offering whatever support they need—training, counseling, time off—they will turn on a dime. They will quickly be back to performing positively.

For example, last month, Patty—who had not sold anything in a couple of months—told me that she was afraid that she would lose her job. She was very upset. I asked her, "How can we help you?" Her response surprised me: she wanted a day off to get her lawn ready for a new swing set for her children, to which I said yes.

I was even more surprised by what happened next. Patty took a day off, came back happily energized, and had her best week of sales in over four months. If I had criticized her, I would have made the situation worse. She was not really upset about work. She was worried about the swing set and her children. It is rarely about work.

Appreciative Leadership is a choice to be positive and to help people, even when they are having a hard time or not performing at their best. It is a choice that awakens the creative spirit in support of collaboration and high performance.

Learn to Talk Story

While working with a leading telecommunication company in Hawaii, we were introduced to the concept of *talk story*. "Great teachers tell stories. They don't lecture about lists of ideas. In Hawaii we call this talk story. Whenever we have something important to say, we say it in a story. It is much more interesting to hear and much easier to remember. Our culture is a story culture. All aspects of our history and culture are passed from generation to generation in stories. We know who we are because we talk story."

We all learn who we are through stories. Traditions—at work and at home—are shared and maintained in story. Think about the stories your first supervisor told you about what it means to work. Or the stories your grandparents told you. Or the stories you've heard around the coffee pot at work recently. What have you learned from these stories? One of our clients, the CEO of a major telecommunications company had this realization about stories, "That means that our organization culture is the stories we tell ourselves about ourselves, and then we forget they are stories." He went on to say, "Then, to change our culture we need to change our stories."[3]

Stories are inspiring. They invite deep listening, respect, and learning. Some stories inspire change. Drawing on the work of Lev Vygotsky,[4] the narrative therapist Michael White points out that stories stimulate change when they are within a range of proximal development.[5] That is, if a story is either too similar or too different from people's current reality, it will not inspire them or move them to action. A similar story does not offer a new vision or give hope; a story that is too different creates anxiety. In neither case do people feel drawn to live into the new narrative. Appreciative Leadership inspires with stories that resonate with people's values, draw on their strengths, and guide them toward a more life-affirming future.

One person's story is the path to another's future. This is no more apparent than with the adoption of technology. iPhone users are a great example: airports, restaurants, and hotel lobbies are full of people talking across aisles, sharing stories, and demonstrating how their favorite applications work. Sharing stories of success readily leads to the adoption of new practices. In another example, consider two friends who migrated from PCs to Mac computers at the same time. Regularly, they shared stories of their new accomplishments. One researched and learned a series of shortcuts. Now they both know and use them. The other shared how she was using the calendar function, and her friend adopted the practice. Learning from another's stories of success is fun and a whole lot easier than going it alone.

Hearing other people's stories enriches our sense of possibility and builds confidence to face uncertainty. Knowing that someone, or some other group, has already accomplished something that we desire gives hope that we too might accomplish it. It inspires bold dreaming and takes the fear out of risky action. Other people's stories inspire us personally as well as at work.

When her doctor told her she had bone cancer, Karen felt as if someone had drawn a dark curtain over her life. She was only 24 years old and had never felt so helpless. She didn't know what to think or what to do. Over the next several weeks, many people shared the stories of their illnesses with her. Their empathy comforted her. Most importantly, their stories of how they had regained their health and gone on to live happy productive lives, inspired her and gave her hope. Over time, she came to believe this could happen to her too. Stories of health and healing give hope and inspire well-being. At work, stories of success, productivity, and collaboration inspire high performance.

Remember: human systems learn, grow, and move in the direction of what they study—the stories they repeatedly tell themselves and each other.

Think about the stories that surround you. What stories do people tell about your team, organization, or community? What story do you wish they were telling? As you read this chapter, imagine what might inspire them to tell a more life-affirming, more hopeful story.

Appreciation: The Fuel of High Performance

Appreciation, a free and available source of inspiration, is underutilized in many organizations and communities. We asked members of three different departments at a major health center what they wanted more of at work. They all said, the feeling of being valued. People want to be valued for who they are and what they do. And yet many leaders and managers are of the opinion that giving appreciation is not in their job description. Does this sound familiar? "Why should I say thank you to people for doing their job?" It is an old paradigm that still pervades the workplace: a demoralizing and dehumanizing perspective that smothers the creative spirit.

Appreciative Leadership is generous with appreciation. Sincere words of encouragement make a positive difference. One focus group participant shared this experience:

Having been absent from the workforce for 14 years to raise my children, I took a job as a part-time coordinator for a very prestigious organization. I felt totally out of my league, but I really wanted to do a good job. It was the end of my very first day on the job, and I was walking to my car when one of the board members—a very well known and respected leader—came up to me and complimented me on how I had handled a situation in a meeting. I remember thinking, "I guess I *can* do this job." I'll never forget it. His sincere words of encouragement were pivotal to my success there.

As this story suggests, letting people know you value them in turn, value themselves. Spontaneous appreciation can have a lasting positive impact.

Establishing regular times and processes for peer appreciation is another practice for inspiring high performance and unleashing positive power. We heard many creative ideas during our research. Here are two that you can easily adapt and use with your team or department:

- We created what we call a *kudos corner*. It is a time on the agenda during our weekly staff meetings when everyone nominates people who went above and beyond that week. We publicly thank them during the meeting, and then we privately thank them after the meeting. It's great because it has spread beyond our meetings to include spontaneous compliments—which are so much more common now than in the past.
- Across departments, we celebrate our hiring anniversaries. Before someone's anniversary, we circulate a card. Everyone signs it and writes something they appreciate about the person. On the anniversary day, we all gather. We each read what we wrote to honor the person, and then we give him or her the card. This tradition really fosters collaboration among our different departments and helps keep the company together.

In every one of the focus groups we conducted, people told stories of being inspired by creative and meaningful recognition. Stories of inspiration were not about large sums of money or big promotions. Instead, they were stories of surprise and creativity in the way people were appreciated. It is clear—creative appreciation fosters high performance. The more creative you are in giving appreciation, formally or informally, the more it will be remembered and taken to heart. And the more likely it is to have a positively powerful impact.

We can all learn from Sean, who coaches girls' softball. On the last day of the season, he called the team together for an awards ceremony. Everybody on the team got an award. He had studied the season's statistics and created awards that were both fun and meaningful. With the best overall batting average, Katy was given a certificate that read "Slugger." Stephanie had the most base hits, so hers read "Steady." But perhaps the sweetest award went to Hannah. "When Hannah came to us, she had never played softball before," said Sean, "But you never would have known that. She had the second highest batting average and the second highest on-base average; and she was a steady outfielder who could both catch and throw." With that, he handed her a certificate that read "Rookie of the Year." Who cared if she was the only rookie on the team? He had seen and acknowledged her strengths, and he had honored her as a full contributor to the team's success.

Appreciative Leadership expresses and reinforces values through recognition. People are inspired by acknowledgment and appreciation. To some degree, we all perform for it. Giving recognition tells people: "What you are doing is good. Keep it up." Appreciation is an inspiring practice for setting expectations and conveying your values. What you acknowledge, appreciate, and reward tells people what matters to you; and it further inspires them to act in accordance.

A great example comes from Maurice Monette and Jeff Jackson. As they approached their twentieth marriage anniversary, they used Appreciative Inquiry to explore what was best in their lives and what they wanted more of in the future. In doing this process, they realized that their relationship was a primary inspiration for the community service work they did. They couldn't imagine contributing as much as one as they do as two. Wondering how to support and inspire other partners, they created the "2×2 Re-create the World Award." Each year the Vallarta Institute, their coaching and consulting organization, awards $2,222.22 to a pair that exemplifies the power of two. Jackson and Monette articulated this foundational value when presenting their first award: "For us the award is a small and hopefully inspiring way to thank others who have also experienced and demonstrated the power that any two people have to make a positive difference in the world.

Now in its fifth award year, they have already recognized the following pairs:

- A Cuban and U.S. pair of authors[6] that collaborated with 12 other authors to write "Cultures of Participation at Work in Cuba and the United States,"[7] demonstrating grassroots professional collaboration in an environment of high-level political conflict
- A reproductive health leader in Ethiopia and a university professor in Mexico who never met but whose paths crossed in how they approached their respective work
- Two married couples in Chile who have built leadership among rural farm families
- A deceased National Painter of Mexico and his artist daughter, who continues her father's legacy by converting their family home into an art and theater workshop for poor children

Appreciative Leadership holds all people in high regard and on a regular basis finds ways to appreciate them and their contributions. While it may not be explicitly stated in your job description at work, it is implicitly stated in the operating instructions for being human: Appreciation is the fuel of high performance. It inspires people to give their best and contribute to the good of the whole; and it stimulates health and emotional well-being. Table 6-1 summarizes seven reasons to give appreciation generously.

TABLE 6-1
SEVEN REASONS TO BE GENEROUS WITH APPRECIATION

1.	Recognition lets people know they are on the right track.
2.	Appreciation communicates and reinforces your values.
3.	Compliments foster a positive emotional environment.
4.	Gratitude is a verbal immune boost; it is good for your health.
5.	Praise is good for the health of those you honor.
6.	Acknowledgment creates a sense of safety.
7.	Gratitude encourages risk taking and experimentation.

 Create a weekly *appreciation checklist* and use it. Make a list of people you appreciate right now. They may be colleagues, staff, and/or family members. Make a note of what you value about them and when you will tell them.

Inspiration takes courage: to explore and discover your hopes and dreams for the future, and to put them into action. And appreciation is one practice for courageously letting people, and the world, know what matters to you and for inspiring others to help achieve it.

Visionary Liveliness

A VISION THAT IS NOT CLEAR IS NOT A VISION AT ALL.

Appreciative Leadership creates a sense of visionary liveliness throughout an organization or community. As the Book of Proverbs tells us, "Where there is no vision, the people perish."[8] Healthy groups, organizations, and communities are known by the vitality of their shared vision for the future. Visions, or compelling images of the future, afford members a sense of positive possibility, give meaning to their lives, and guide their activities. Once expressed, a vision, dream, or positive intent seeks the path to its fulfillment. Visionary liveliness unleashes movement toward a better way. It points the way to positive transformation.

While a leader or a team of leaders may have a vision, it is not the vision itself that matters. It is the way the vision moves through the organization that makes a difference. It is the degree to which it evokes visionary liveliness by permeating conversations, relationships, and performance that matters. The following story illustrates how one, simple and clear vision made a positive difference for employees and customers:

Qwest Communications employees were demoralized. The company was billions of dollars in debt, and some members of its former leadership team were under criminal investigation. The level of employee embarrassment and shame was so high that many technicians wore their own clothes to and from work, changing into company uniforms only on the job.

Recognizing the need for vision, renewed pride, and visible change, the new CEO declared, "We can't fix what's behind us. We can only tackle what's ahead." He put forth a simple and very meaningful vision: focus on customers. He introduced a new company brand, "Spirit of Service,"[9] saying that it called employees to see the world through the eyes of the customer, to take ownership of customer concerns, and to create relationships with customers instead of passing their problems along to someone else. And he gave employees permission to do whatever it takes to meet the needs of customers.

Initially employees were skeptical, even cynical, but he was unwavering. In all of his communications, he mentioned "customer focus," often sharing stories and acknowledging people for outstanding customer service. Little by little, people embraced the vision in their everyday work. Most thrived in the new environment and became proud of what they did and where they worked. Within a year, thousands of employees had purchased more than $1 million of company-branded clothing. A transformation had indeed taken place. Two years later, customers weighed in. J.D. Power and Associates awarded the company's technicians the highest customer satisfaction rating in the industry.

People need vision. The good news is that a vision does not have to be your own vision to make a difference. It can be yours; or better yet, it can be a shared vision. A vision that is collectively created has more momentum for action than one created by a few people at the top and rolled out to others. Both Martin Luther King, Jr., and U.S. President William Clinton defined leadership as being in service to the future that is most desired by the people they served. As such, they displayed a leadership style often described as "Finding a parade and getting in front of it."

The leadership team of the Sisters of the Good Shepherd's newly formed Province of Mid-North America (PMNA) led according to the same ideal. Soon after a merger of four provinces, they used Appreciative Inquiry to engage nearly 650 people in interviews and dialogue, resulting in the articulation of a fully agreed upon and compelling shared vision, mission, and statements of strategic direction.[10] In so doing, they created a palpable sense of visionary liveliness among their community of 250 Sisters and the leaders and staff of their ministries.

You know what it feels like when people are inspired, and the creative spirit is alive, well and thriving in your organization. Visionary liveliness is exciting, fun, and highly productive. You also know what it is like when it is missing—when there is a leadership vacuum. One focus group participant shared this story:

For nearly five years, the company was run by a bully. The CEO was a tyrant who belittled everyone with whom he came into contact. Nothing was ever good enough for him. No one would dare make a move or bring a new idea forward for fear of his anger and criticism.

When his departure was announced, employees cheered. And then the new leader arrived. He was likable, but not engaged. It was not unusual to see him nod off in meetings. His direct reports were given free reign to run their departments. Silos sprouted and morale plummeted to its lowest ever. His lack of vision and engagement with us was just as deflating as the critical leadership we had lived with for so long.

Appreciative Leadership kindles visionary liveliness by engaging with people in inquiry and conversations about hopes and dreams for the future. In the process, visions—compelling images of the future—emerge that awaken the creative spirit, inspire hope, and generate inspired actions. As the following story illustrates a shared vision or compelling image of the future can help a group transcend competition and generate a creative platform for collaboration:

The leadership team of the human resources department of a major pharmaceutical company had gathered for a team building. The session began with the group of six people—one VP and five directors—sharing high-point stories and dreams for the future. As they shared their dreams for their own futures, a deep silence filled the room. All of the five directors had the same dream: to become vice president of human resources. At first panic set in; after all, there was only one VP position and their boss was not ready to relinquish it.

And even if he were ready to retire, only one of them would get his job. The competition they felt among themselves was now explicit and made sense.

As they talked openly about what seemed like an impossible reality, light bulbs went on. They all had enough experience to be VPs. They were all competent enough to be VPs. There were plenty of VP jobs to be had—in other divisions of their company and even in other companies. What if one of their shared goals was to all become VPs within the next three years? What if they supported each other rather than competed with each other? What if they became the best human resources department in the pharmaceutical industry—a pool of the best executive leadership talent available? Their personal dreams converged and became one big collective dream. And so it was that over the next three years they all supported one other so that one team member successfully started her own company, while the other four directors all became HR VPs in other divisions and other companies.

So what makes a vision compelling? What stimulates visionary liveliness? In a landmark essay, "Positive Image, Positive Action," Professor David Cooperrider summarizes research in fields from education to medicine to athletics to sociology, all indicating that positive images of the future inspire positive action:

Cancer survivors use . . . [visualization] to enter states that enable their bodies to perform, like those of athletes, at levels beyond the ordinary. People in pain use it to manage and control discomfort. Nicholas Hall, a physician at the George Washington Medical Center, found that patients using visualization increased their number of circulating white blood cells, and also levels of a hormone important to auxiliary white cells. He found that visualization worked best when patients chose their own images and were able to see them as clearly as if looking with their physical eyes. A child with cancer successfully imagined it as a big, dumb, gray lump that he repeatedly "shot" with a rocket ship. Within a year he was cured.[11]

Athletes have long recognized the powerful role that images play in human performance. Golf icon Jack Nicklaus has described how he consciously visualizes the "perfect" shot in order to enhance his performance. Indeed, he has said that the difference between good golfers and great golfers is the capacity to focus on the image of success:

I never hit a shot, not even in practice, without having a very sharp, in-focus picture of it in my head. First I see the ball where I want it to finish, nice and white and sitting up high on the bright green grass. Then the scene quickly changes, and I see the ball going there; its path, trajectory, and shape, even its behavior on landing. Then there is a sort of fade-out, and the next scene shows me making the kind of swing that will turn the previous images into reality.[12]

As the research and examples show, compelling visions are images of the ideal. They are tangible and tactile, engaging the heart, mind, and the body. They breathe life into new possibilities by showing people that their most desired future has been and can be attained. Roger Bannister's ability to break through the four-minute-mile barrier is a classic example of this. At the time, his achievement was hailed as one of the greatest in sports history. But within three years, 16 other runners had achieved the same thing. Today, while laudable, running a mile in under four minutes is not uncommon. It seems the real barrier was a psychological one.

Table 6-2 describes "Five Criteria for a Compelling Vision." Use these criteria to test the inspirational value of your strategic plan, your company's vision or mission statement, and/or your personal development plan.

TABLE 6-2
FIVE CRITERIA FOR A COMPELLING VISION

1.	*It is desired.* A compelling image of the future is something you want. Does your vision, dream, or intention describe—in the affirmative—what people want their future to be? Is it congruent with their collective core values?
2.	*It is inclusive.* A compelling image meets the needs of everyone involved. It transcends the hopes and dreams of individual people and groups. Does your vision, dream, or intention reflect the hopes, dreams, needs, and wants of everyone involved? Is it a shared image for the future?
3.	*It is a believable stretch.* A compelling image is a stretch beyond the status quo, and yet it is within reach. Does your vision, dream, or intention go beyond the bounds of the status quo? Do you also believe it is possible to achieve?
4.	*It requires collaboration.* A compelling image belongs to the whole and requires collaboration in order to be carried out and achieved. Does your vision, dream, or intention depend on others to achieve? Does it stimulate collaboration?
5.	*It requires creativity and innovation.* A compelling image of the future is an innovative alternative to the present. Does your vision, dream, or intention require creativity to be realized?

To strengthen your capacity for inspiration, practice envisioning the world, your workplace, your relationships, and/or your results *as you would have them be.* Visualize and speak of the future in as positive and concrete terms as possible. Invite others to share their hopes and dreams with you, and together create your most enlivening and irresistible vision for a better world.

Give yourself five minutes, now, to envision your ideal world. Visualize it as you would have it be. Make note of what you see.

Hope: More Than a Compelling Vision

Appreciative Leadership inspires people by revealing and amplifying signs of hope. This requires more than just a compelling vision. In her groundbreaking book *Positivity,* Dr. Barbara Fredrickson defines *hope* as "the belief that things can change. No matter how awful or uncertain they are at this moment, things can turn out better. Possibilities exist."[13] Fredrickson's research correlates hope to both satisfaction and performance. With hope, people find satisfaction in what they do, and they do it well. They achieve what they set out to accomplish even in the midst of challenging times.

Hope is a complex, collective emotion that arises in the presence of hardship, disaster, violence, and destruction. It inspires people to align their strengths and to contribute what they can toward a common cause or a shared purpose. It gives them courage and confidence to redefine their lives, learn from their struggles and each other, and coauthor a more life-affirming future. Summarizing the research on hope, Professors Luthans and Avolio describe this as "will power and way power."[14] *Will power* necessitates a compelling vision combined with emotional resources and community support. *Way power* requires that a path forward and tangible resources be apparent. As shown in Figure 6–1, both are essential elements in the formula for hope.

FIGURE 6- 1
FORMULA FOR HOPE

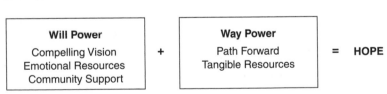

| **Will Power**
Compelling Vision
Emotional Resources
Community Support | + | **Way Power**
Path Forward
Tangible Resources | = | HOPE |

When people see a better way, they want to know both how it will be achieved and how they can contribute. In short, they want a path forward. According to the people we interviewed, having and following a positive path forward gives you hope, and eventually gets you where you want to go. One person said that if you start with a specific vision, then forge and stick with a clear path, people will know where you are going and trust you. Another suggested that the best way to create change without resistance is to create a plan together and do everything gradually. Both approaches illustrate the benefits of a shared path forward: it gets you where you want to go; it builds trust; and it leads to positive change.

You've probably heard the call for a path forward. It sounds like this: "So what happens next?" "When will we get started?" "Who's going to do that?" "When will we meet again?" "I can. . ." "I will. . ., if it is what we need." Embedded in each question is a commitment to go forward and concern about how to do so. Recognizing the need for widespread clarity and agreement, many of our clients find it beneficial to use a template like the one shown in Table 6-3 to document and communicate their Appreciative Path Forward.

Inspiration—the process of generating compelling images and showing the way to a better future—is an unbounded source of positive power. It stimulates hope, liberates energy, and focuses action on behalf of the whole. On a personal level, Appreciative Leadership inspires hope through inquiry and dialogue about dreams and the steps that must be taken to realize them. Hearing other people's hopes for the future is akin to receiving road maps that tell us how to support them.

As captain of the track team, Patrick knew his teammates' hopes and dreams. One person hoped to go to college on a track scholarship. When that dream was jeopardized due to an injury, Patrick took action. It was the two-mile race in the national finals. His teammate was leading when he sprained a muscle; but didn't stop, because he had to finish the race. Patrick saw the path forward. Without missing a beat, he stepped in, grabbed his teammate's arm, and ran the last two laps with him, arm in arm. They finished the race, and his teammate's dream came true. He won the track scholarship to college.

TABLE 6-3 **APPRECIATIVE PATH FORWARD**			

Our compelling vision or purpose:

	Strengths, assets, and resources:		
Will Power	**Opportunities:**	**Aspiration statements:**	
Way Power	**Action steps:**	**Tangible and intangible resources:**	**Timelines:**

When people learn about, see, or hear of a better way, they move toward it. They are stirred to work for it. They want to make it happen. Hope rouses people to action. From athletes who replay winning games over and over in their minds, to volunteers who work selflessly in service of a candidate or a cause, to entrepreneurs who work endless hours to bring their new product to market, to nurses and physicians who daily tend to those in need, the courage of inspiration invites people to greatness.

One of the more inspiring stories of the twentieth century is that of the United Religions Initiative. In a time of war, hunger, and abuse, it is a story of hope: a story of how an inspirational vision and path forward can make a positive difference in the world on a daily basis.

It was the middle of the night in the fall of 1993. William Swing, then bishop of the Episcopal diocese of California, had received a call that day from the United Nations. The institution's fiftieth anniversary was pending, and UN organizers wished to celebrate with an interfaith service in Swing's home church, Grace Cathedral—the site of the original UN charter signing. Swing couldn't sleep. Why, he thought, do political leaders and diplomats spend their lives working for peace, when so many of the world's conflicts are religious in nature? When aren't religious leaders involved?

This night of insomnia proved fateful. Inspired by a vision of a United Nation of religions, Swing embarked on a quest. He convened a global summit—a "Call to Action"—to share his vision and outline the path forward. Over a period of five years, the budding movement expanded its reach, studied and learned from effective global movements, envisioned the future, and designed systems and structures. The United Religions Initiative (URI) was chartered in 2000 in Pittsburgh, Pennsylvania. Its purpose statement has become a beacon in a world torn apart by religious hatred: "to promote enduring, daily interfaith cooperation; to end religiously motivated violence; and to create cultures of peace, justice, and healing for the Earth and all living beings."

Today, the United Religious Initiative serves people in 72 countries through a network of 450 local "Cooperation Circles" and multiregion clusters. Including outreach for youth and children, environmental projects, economic development, peace building, and works on HIV/AIDS, it also serves as an educational hub for people seeking information about world religions and peace building. In countless ways, it is making the world a better place, one relationship at a time.

The birth of the URI vividly illustrates how inspiration can chart the course for powerful, positive results. Indeed, new products, processes and partnerships—new ways of living, working, and being—inevitably spring forth in the presence of a compelling, hopeful images and a clear path forward. By inspiring hope for a better world, Appreciative Leadership evokes its realization.

The Reenchantment of Work

We believe work to be a noble endeavor. We are fortunate enough to like our work and the people, colleagues, and clients with whom we work. We see the connections between what we do and the way it benefits people and the planet. Our work affords us opportunities for meaningful relationships, for the expression of our strengths, for creativity, and for learning—as well as providing for our basic needs. We realize that this is not the case for everyone. We believe, however, that it is the potential for everyone.

It is the call of Appreciative Leadership to make it so: to foster the reenchantment of work, so that people's work provides for their basic needs and enables them to feel proud of their contribution to the well-being of the whole. Friends Ashwani Khurana and Dinesh Chandra embarked upon a bold experiment to do just so in India:

Ashwani—CEO of K & Company, India's largest privately owned lottery company—and Dinesh—who teaches that business is a place for personal growth and transformation—together created what they call a "consciousness organization." In so doing, they elevated the work, the lives, and the legacy of hundreds of people working in K & Company. It began when they met. Ashwani, a self-made man who had been ridiculed by school friends for his family's involvement in the lottery business, told Dinesh of his passion for the environment. He wanted to become known as "Mr. Tree." His dream was to create an organization in which people were motivated to work not just because they needed to but because they were learning, growing, and contributing to something meaningful—planting and caring for trees throughout the city.

Ashwani and Dinesh aligned their strengths to create an inspired work community: an interdependent group of people whose love and service for the environment would enrich their own lives, help the environment, and further the economic friendliness of the business. They engaged employees in an active learning process aimed at transforming compliance into creativity.

"The results," in Dinesh's words, "have been tremendous. Office boys (*peons* as they are called in the local lingua) began taking on more meaningful jobs: filing, answering the phone and talking with customers, faxing, and learning about and using computers. They have enjoyed this work and their self-esteem has increased. Along with company drivers, they have planted and cared for trees along the roadsides and in local parks, further instilling in them a sense of belonging and love for the environment." And the business is going strong.

People long to be inspired—by the possibility of high ideals, by learning, by the selfless dedication of other people, and by moments of collaboration that make a positive difference. They want to be part of a team, work group, organization, or community whose elevated purpose calls them to apply their strengths and to give their best. They want their work to be enchanting. They want it to invite them into a world of wonder, learning, and meaningful contribution.

In the words of Antoine de Saint-Exupery, "If you want to build a ship, don't drum up people to collect wood and don't assign them tasks and work, but rather teach them to long for the endless immensity of the sea."[15] The many people with whom we talked do not yearn to be motivated or micromanaged; they yearn to be appreciated and engaged in meaningful, uplifting, enlivening ways that serve the good of the whole.

Motivation is a mechanistic metaphor applied to human performance. It refers to both positive and negative practices: the carrot and the stick. While both can powerfully influence human behavior, they are not both positively powerful. Negative motivational practices such as criticism, threats, and punishments stimulate fear, compliance, and low self-esteem. They are diminishing. They stifle potential and tend to be destructive rather than socially constructive.

Anna was absolutely thrilled to begin her new job with a well-regarded national social profit organization. Finally, she was getting to do what she loved and get paid for it. On her first day she completed the necessary paperwork for new hires, and she was escorted to the CEO's office by the HR manager. The CEO looked up from the papers on his desk and said gruffly, "Don't screw it up." Anna was stunned. She walked away wondering why she had been hired and whether or not she wanted to work there after all.

Positive motivational practices, on the other hand, are inspirational. There is a saying, "A good life is counted not by how many breaths you take, but by how many experiences you have that take your breath away." So it is with inspiration. It gives people pause. It causes them to stop, take a deep breath, and realize they are on the right track. It gives them a sense that they are part of something bigger and more meaningful than themselves. The story of the three stonemasons illustrates this well:

Three stonemasons were busy working when a stranger wandered by. The first stonemason was toting rocks to a pile, near a wall. "What are you doing?" said the stranger.

The stonemason replied, "Can't you see that I'm carrying rocks?"

The stranger asked the second laborer, "What are you doing?"

"I'm building a wall," he replied.

A few steps away, the stranger came upon a third mason. "What are you doing?" he asked.

This worker smiled. "I'm building a cathedral to the glory of God!"[16]

You can tell the difference between an enchanted, inspired workplace and a disenchanted workplace by the language you hear. Inspiration shows up along with words and feelings that describe positive human experiences: awareness, ah-ha's, beauty, epiphany, hope, wonder, possibility, potential, and fun! Words create worlds. The habitual language of business renders the creative spirit invisible. An artifact of command-and-control leadership, it is intended to ensure order rather than liberate creativity.

Read the following list of common business words: *administration, memorandum, quarterly report, economic indicator, timeline, sales quota, strategic plan, risk management, budget,* and *human resources.* How do they make you feel?

People are stimulated by the use of elevated language that speaks to the whole person—mind, body, heart, and spirit. Poets and playwrights know this, and so do appreciative leaders. They use language, words, and stories that resonate with the heart and open the mind: for meaning making among people, as a vehicle for stimulating collective wisdom, and for elevating collective consciousness.

Our research suggests that it takes love to create an inspired workplace, to create an environment where people flourish. People can tell if you love what you are doing, and with whom you are working. They want leadership that cares, that leads with love.

> I had a mentor who believed in me from day 1. He helped me see things in such a way that I wanted to be a better person. He had such a heart! His advice to me was, "If you are going to be a leader, you'd better love people." His encouragement drew people to him like a bee to a flower. And he was not afraid to tell you what you needed to hear. He could do it in such a way that you accepted it. He truly loved people, and it made him a great leader.

The ultimate Appreciative Leadership challenge is to love what you do and with whom you work. When you do, everything else will follow in a good and meaningful way.

Organizing to a Life-Affirming Purpose

Inspiration abides among people. It activates energy, confidence, and hope. Most significantly, however, it points the way to a better life. Inspiration is evoked when people share stories of success, use elevated language, and paint compelling visions of the future. The most courageous and transformative Appreciative Leadership practices are those that make it possible, indeed inevitable, for people to organize around a life-affirming purpose. Consider, for example, Green Mountain Coffee Roasters, whose inspirational mission is "Brewing a Better World." Their Web site states this purpose:

> We believe a whole systems approach is the most effective business model, and we are truly motivated by helping create a more sustainable world… The ultimate coffee experience is one that makes a positive difference in every life we touch from tree to cup. Naturally, coffee lovers are better off for having a great cup of Green Mountain Coffee; yet it goes further than that: a woman who picks coffee in

Mexico gets prenatal care; a co-op in Indonesia receives a price premium and gains new market access after achieving Fair Trade and organic certification; and alternative energy projects across the United States get infusions of capital.[17]

Thanks to the inspirational organization created by Bob Stiller and his highly inclusive team, everyone involved with Green Mountain Coffee—from growers to drinkers—supports the well-being of the whole planet.

Making it possible for people to organize to a life-affirming purpose most often requires the redesign of processes and systems. This takes courage to see the realities of the world and creativity to design processes to transcend them. Social entrepreneurs around the world are doing just this. For example, Nobel Peace Prize winner Professor Muhammad Yunus redesigned the structure of banking, making it possible for people to get loans without collateral through the Grameen Bank.[18]

Similarly, Albina Ruiz founded Ciudad Saludable because government-run garbage collection in Peru had not been effective, and illegal dumping was causing environmental deterioration and groundwater contamination. Ruiz set out to break that cycle. In addition to taking care of the garbage problem, her microenterprise model has provided self-employment opportunities to local residents in neighborhoods where unemployment rates have been high. The businesses have often been run by women who go door to door collecting garbage and fees, and educating people about respecting and protecting their environment. Some women have even built profitable businesses by creating products like organic fertilizer out of the trash they have collected.[19]

The list of businesses and social profit organizations designed to transcend the realities of today's world, provide access to food, clothing, and shelter, and create well-being across the planet is growing daily. To learn more about how appreciative leaders around the world are organizing for a life-affirming purpose, we recommend the Business as an Agent of World Benefit (BAWB)[20] initiative at Case Western Reserve University. How might you redesign your business, community, agency, or processes to become an agent of world benefit?

Enhancing Your Capacity:
Resources for Further Development

	Key Practices	Page Numbers
TABLE 6–4 **INSPIRATION: A SUMMARY OF KEY PRACTICES**		
Personal	• Choose to be positive.	128
	• Talk story.	131
One-to-one	• Be generous with appreciation.	133
	• Share hopes and dreams for the future.	137
Team or group	• Foster hope by planning the path forward.	146
	• Reenchant your workplace.	148
Whole organization or community	• Organize to a life-affirming purpose.	152

Recommended Books

Banker to the Poor: Micro-Lending and the Battle Against World Poverty by Muhammad Yunus and Alan Jolis (New York: PublicAffairs), 2003.

Joy, Inspiration and Hope by Verena Kast and translated by Douglas Whitcher (College Station: Texas A&M University Press), 2004.

Maps of Narrative Practice by Michael White (New York: Norton), 2007.

Recommended Web Sites

Green Mountain Coffee
www.greenmountaincoffee.com
The values-driven manufacturer and distributor of organic, fair trade, and specialty gourmet coffees, Green Mountain Coffee Roasters creatively and effectively inspires its workforce, customers, and partners to "do well by doing good."

The New Heroes
www.pbs.org/opb/thenewheroes
The New Heroes tells the dramatic stories of 14 daring "social entreprencurs" from all corners of the globe who develop innovations that bring life-changing tools and resources to people desperate for viable solutions.

Ode Magazine
http://www.odemagazine.com/
Ode is a print and online publication about positive news, and the people and ideas that are changing our world for the better. Founded in the spring of 1995 in Rotterdam, the Netherlands, as an alternative to mainstream publications—a magazine that was open to new inspirations and new visions from around the world—its aims are to bring a new reality into view and to explore opportunities for positive change in our daily lives and our daily minds.

Vallarta Institute
www.vallartainstitute.com
The Vallarta Institute *recreates* more of what works best for individuals, work teams, and communities. Associates provide consulting, coaching, and facilitation services on site, over the phone, and/or at the inspirational Vallarta Institute Retreat Center in Puerto Vallarta, Mexico.

SEVEN

The Path of Integrity: Making Choices for the Good of the Whole

I 'RATTED' ON MYSELF

The Appreciative Inquiry advisory team meeting started, as always, with an appreciative check-in. The 35 members, a microcosm of the whole health system—physicians, nurses, medical school faculty, students, hospital administrators, human resources managers, communication specialists, executives, and line staff—were taking turns sharing stories. Each person was answering the question, "What have you seen, heard, or experienced since we last met one month ago that tells you that the organization is indeed changing for the better?"

When it was Mary's turn, she began by saying, "I just have to tell you, I am really proud and happy to work here. I have had an unusually hard week because last week

I made a medical error. Fortunately, no one was harmed. So I took a risk, and I reported it to our quality and safety team. I 'ratted' on myself; and I've been afraid all week that I would lose my job. Even though I went to the training and heard it said over and over that under our new policy there will be no negative consequences if we report errors, I just didn't believe it until today. I want to read from the e-mail I received this morning." She began:

"Dear Mary, Thank you for reporting the error you made last week. We too are happy that no one was harmed. We are especially grateful to you for reporting it. As you know, our new policy is based on two beliefs: One, over the course of a day, a week, a month, or a year, we all make mistakes. And, two, quality care and safety for our patients and our staff, at all levels, depends on all of us being transparent with our errors. Thank you for having the courage and integrity to do so."

The e-mail went on to describe what would happen next: how the report would be handled, who would review it, and what they would do as a result. It listed a number of changes that had already been made based on other people's quality reports.

Not only was Mary not going to lose her job, she was being informed about steps being taken to improve quality and safety throughout the whole health system—something she obviously cared about enough to risk her job and her career.

Appreciative Leadership begins and ends with integrity. When you are on the path of integrity, people know it. They follow your ideas and ideals. They model their ways of working after yours. And they contribute their best to the ideals you put forth.

When you are off the path of integrity, people sense it. They see it in your actions—when the way you relate to people minimizes them, belittles them, or even harms them. They hear it in your words and the tone of your voice—when you make promises you cannot deliver upon. They feel it—when you are short on emotional intelligence, avoid conflict, blame others, or express anger inappropriately. When you are off the path of integrity, people move away from your ideas, your way of working and you. They seek out others whom they can respect. When you are off the path of integrity, you become a role model for what not to do. People learn and perform in spite of you.

Integrity refers to a myriad of relational practices. When the people we interviewed talked about the presence or absence of integrity, they described it with words such as honesty, transparency, moral and ethical conduct, speaking truth to power, making and keeping commitments, open communication, congruity of words and deeds, reconciliation, forgiveness, and authenticity. All these notions point to the idea that *integrity means wholeness*. Appreciative Leadership stays on the path of integrity by making choices that serve the whole. Any time your thoughts, words, and deeds bring greater wholeness to people and groups, you are on the path of integrity. For example, when you help people discover their strengths and fulfill their dreams, you are supporting their wholeness. When you include people in conversations and collaborations that bridge social divides, you are enhancing organization and community wholeness. When you take care of yourself and work to your strengths, you are nurturing your own wholeness. And when you design sustainability into the processes, products, and services of your organization, you are contributing to the integral well-being of the whole planet.

In the early 1990s we were invited to facilitate the design and establishment of a global interfaith organization. It was a formidable task involving hundreds of religious and spiritual leaders and scholars from around the world—most of whom did not know each other. As we discussed how we would know we had succeeded, our colleague Dr. David Cooperrider suggested that we focus on the quality of conversations and their impact on relationships.

There are three kinds of leadership conversations:

- Relationship-canceling conversations
- Relationship-tolerating conversations
- Relationship-enhancing conversations

Only relationship-enhancing conversations move people and groups toward wholeness.

Relationship-canceling conversations occur within all arenas of work and life, including interfaith communities. You know what they sound like: "They should not be allowed to participate because they are not a sanctioned sorority, a true religion, or a taxpayer." "We don't need to include IT, radiology, or HR. It is not in their job description, and they will only confuse the issue anyway." Relationship-canceling conversations include name-calling, blaming, and belittling. They include any of the ways people and groups are made invisible, deemed insignificant, and excluded from relationship.

Relationship-tolerating conversations allow for the existence of other people and groups as long as they maintain their "place." Relationship-tolerating conversations do not even hint at the desire for meaningful relationships. You probably know people who say things like: "My neighbors are ... and they don't create any trouble for us. We welcome them in our church, on our team, in the department. We just don't socialize together." Relationship-tolerating conversations keep other people and groups at a distance. People are depersonalized and tolerated through the use of generalizations and language such as "they" and "them." These conversations do not afford people a sense of belonging. They neither foster community nor create a sense of wholeness.

Relationship-enhancing conversations, on the other hand, strengthen the bonds of relatedness, build community, and give people a deep sense of belonging in a meaningful way. We hope these comments sound familiar to you: "Why don't we ask the kids what they want. After all it is their community park." "These people are new to the company; let's find out what they love about their work, and see what we can learn from them. "Mentors should be cross-departmental in order to build bridges on personal and departmental levels." Relationship-enhancing conversations encourage people to meet and get to know one another. They demonstrate confidence in people and seek to bring out their best. They build and strengthen relationships as a foundation for performance, learning, and resiliency to change. Relationship-enhancing conversations are a positively powerful practice for demonstrating respect, establishing trust, and inspiring unprecedented collaboration in service to the whole—whether it is a whole department, project, organization, community, or the world.

The path of integrity deepens relationships and spans time. When asked, "What is Zen," the Venerable Goto Roshi replied: "Simple, simple, so simple. Infinite gratitude toward all things past; infinite service to all things present; infinite responsibility to all things future."[1] Appreciative Leadership practices are similarly threefold. They foster gratitude for the past. They embody service in the present. And they exemplify responsibility for the future. Your path of integrity has to do with how you learn from, honor, and appreciate the best of what has been. It has to do with the ways you care for the whole of life: yourself, other people, other living beings, and the earth. It has to do with the choices you make: with whom and how you relate, how you balance your needs with those of others, and how you generate, use, and care for resources. And it has to do with the impact of your thoughts, words, and deeds—the legacy you leave for generations to come.

In Service to the Whole

To be on the path of integrity is to be moving, growing, and evolving toward wholeness; and to be supporting and enabling others to do the same. Appreciative Leadership attends to wholeness on many levels: seeking the whole story, aligning the whole organization, caring for the whole world, applying holistic approaches, and being open to the "holy." Appreciative Leadership seeks the *whole story*. By inviting, being open to, and sincerely listening to all voices, collective wisdom—the sense of the whole—emerges. People want leadership to listen to their personal ideas, thoughts, and feelings. More significantly, however, they want leadership to attend to the voice of the whole. Drs. Diana Whitney and David Cooperrider have written, "The experience of wholeness satisfies the human need to be part of a larger community, to feel like you belong. It establishes trust among different people and credibility in outcomes. When everyone is part of a decision, you know it will stick."[2] As Whitney and Cooperrider suggest, public conversations that reveal the "whole story" engender commitment and shared responsibility.

Appreciative Leadership demonstrates integrity by ensuring the alignment of the *whole organization*. It makes certain that purpose, principles, practices, priorities, and processes are congruent throughout the entire organization. People want leadership that walks the talk. They want leadership teams that espouse, live, and lead with a shared set of values, a shared leadership style, and a shared approach to human development and change. People want the "logos, ethos, and pathos" of the organization to make sense together. They want the strategic plan to make sense in the industry and to be congruent with the marketing plan, the way customers are treated, and the way resources are disbursed. They want everyone in all departments, functions, and levels of the organization to be held accountable to the same work ethic. In short, they want to respect the whole of the organization. They want to feel that they belong to an integrated whole that is larger and more positively powerful than any one person or group.

Processes that create whole-system alignment also advance organizational agility and flexibility. Paradoxically, they also establish a strong culture, and generate the collective capacity for positive change. When members of an organization or community gather regularly to consciously discuss and align their strategies, systems, and structures, they build relationships, develop collaborate capabilities, and foster the commitment needed for large-scale change. Appreciative Leadership attends to the balance of stability and change; the need for whole-system alignment and agility; and the need for a strong organizational culture that embodies the willingness to change.

Integrity is about the *whole world*—thinking globally and acting locally. Appreciative Leadership, wherever it is and whatever its purpose, holds a broad view. It is mindful of long- and short-term forces; global and local forces; and human, ecological, technical, and financial forces. The path of integrity includes practices to bring competing, conflicting, and/or contradicting forces into awareness and harmony through inquiry, dialogue, and collective reflection.

Appreciative Leadership is life centric, holding all living beings in positive regard. It establishes priorities and engages with others to design and build social habits, processes, and institutions that are life affirming and sustainable. It uses resources—communication, money, technology, education, and social networks—to further the well-being of the whole. For example, the Business as an Agent of World Benefit (BAWB) initiative at Case Western Reserve University serves as a forum for online and face-to-face information sharing and learning among members of organizations dedicated to global sustainability. It highlights the courage, creativity, and collaboration needed to design organizations and communities today to ensure the well-being of tomorrow.

Appreciative Leadership employs *holistic approaches* involving mind, body, emotions, and spirit to engage diverse groups of people, to support the authentic expression of human potential, and to foster the design of life-affirming products, services, and organizations. Intuition, silence, appreciative check-ins, training in emotional intelligence, sabbaticals, slow meetings, meditation, improbable pairs, and ceremonies are some of the many practices available to create and nurture a life-giving workplace.

Wholeness is also about *holy*—the sacred life force that moves through and around us all. Joseph Jaworski, CEO of the American Leadership Forum has said:

> All human beings are part of that unbroken whole which is continually unfolding from the implicate and making itself manifest in our explicate world. One of the most important roles we can play individually and collectively is to create an opening, or to "listen" to the implicate order unfolding, and

then to create dreams, visions, and stories that we sense at
our center want to happen—that as Buber said, "want to be
actualized ... with human spirit and deed."[3]

Diana Whitney calls this "spiritual resonance" and suggests that
it "occurs when people working together share a purpose that is at
the same time both task oriented and spiritually oriented. It occurs
when people truly honor each other as well as nature as living beings,
and when they do their best to care for all life. It occurs when people
recognize vulnerabilities and strengths and work in ways that bring
out the best of people, personally and collectively. Most significantly,
spiritual resonance is a collective spiritual experience."[4]

Appreciative Leadership advances "spirituality in the workplace."
The Tyson Center for Faith and Spirituality in the Workplace at the
Sam M. Walton College of Business at the University of Arkansas is
a source of more information on this subject. The center's mission is
to advance the state of research, practice, and teaching in the field
of faith and spirituality in the workplace. It serves as a resource for
business leaders, academics, spiritual and faith leaders, and practitioners. Programs cover topics such as principles for incorporating faith,
religion, and spirituality in the workplace along with stories of how
exemplary organizations are integrating them.[5]

Along the path of integrity, Appreciative Leadership encounters
many choices, among them: whom to hire, promote, or fire; where and
with whom to do business; how to determine fees, costs, and budgets;
how to allocate resources; how to balance work and family needs; and
how to be a good parent, partner, colleague, and leader. The issues facing leadership today are seldom simple, and the path of integrity may
not be readily apparent. Appreciative Leadership's positively powerful
approach is to engage with others and together, to make decisions for
the good of the whole.

Working in service to the whole may mean going against dominant
social structures, even those that you earlier believed in and supported.
When necessary, appreciative leaders take a stand against habitual social

processes and antiquated institutions that belittle people, are unjust, or that cause divisiveness and injury. President Jimmy Carter did just this in July 2009, when after 60 years as a devoted member, he made the painful and difficult decision to "sever my ties with the Southern Baptist Convention." In his letter entitled "Losing My Religion for Equality," he went on to say

> It was, however, an unavoidable decision when the convention's leaders, quoting a few carefully selected Bible verses and claiming that Eve was created second to Adam and was responsible for original sin, ordained that women must be "subservient" to their husbands and prohibited from serving as deacons, pastors, or chaplains in the military service. ...
>
> At its most repugnant, the belief that women must be subjugated to the wishes of men excuses slavery, violence, forced prostitution, genital mutilation, and national laws that omit rape as a crime. But is also costs many millions of girls and women control over their own bodies and lives, and continues to deny them fair access to education, health, employment, and influence within their own communities. ... The justification of discrimination against women and girls on grounds of religion or tradition, as if it were prescribed by a Higher Authority, is unacceptable.[6]

President Carter's decision suggests that Appreciative Leadership forgo the *righteousness of the rules* and instead give voice to life-affirming values and the need for a more just, caring, and sustainable world. The phrase "think globally, act locally" suggests how best to contribute to the whole: be aware of the global realities of our time, be clear about your values and principles, hold each and every person in positive regard, and take a stand within your own domain of power to create a world that works for all. This means change: a set of future-oriented priorities, the establishment of appreciative ways of working, and the design of life-affirming structures, systems, products, and services. Appreciative Leadership is uniquely suited to the task of systemic positive change.

Conscious Decision Making

We live and work in a world created by the choices we make personally, collectively, and globally. As the following story illustrates, every decision you make is an opportunity to demonstrate your values, to put your principles into action, and to contribute to the sustainability of the planet:

> I worked with the executive team of a leading international health care company for over a decade. They were then, and continue to be, one of my "role model" executive teams and organizations. I remember asking the CEO and the vice president of people why the culture change process we were facilitating was so important to them. Their answers stay with me to this day: "This is the best way we know to make a better world. We believe in our business and want it to grow and be strong. But more significantly, we hold the decisions we take as leaders to a high standard. We have a responsibility to help people serve the world in meaningful ways. This helps them feel valued, it supports their growth, and it helps the world become a better place. We are clear about our values, and we want to be sure they are embodied in all we do. That's the only way we can live and work with integrity."
>
> That was an ah-ha moment for me! They were creating the world they wanted to live in by making their organization the kind of place in which they and others would want to work. For them it was a simple equation—know your values, imagine the world you want to live in, and create it in all you do day by day. Now that is conscious decision making.

The path of integrity unfolds with the decisions you make. It is the trail you leave as the impacts of your decisions ripple outward. Each and every day you make hundreds of decisions. And every decision you make emerges from and influences the interconnected web of all life. Test this idea for yourself.

 Scan the past couple of hours in your mind:

- *How many decisions have you made?* To call someone, to answer the phone, to write e-mails, to order lunch, to cancel a subscription, to schedule a meeting, to take a day off, to meet with your team, to have a cup of coffee.

- *How many decisions have you talked about and contributed to making?* The agenda for the meeting, the timing of the new product launch, the budget for marketing, the purchase of new technology, the strategy for culture change.

- *How many decisions occurred, in this same hour, that impacted you, your work, or your family?* A colleague resigned, a large order was placed with your company, the price of gasoline increased, you were invited to speak at a conference next year, your spouse went shopping for dinner, violence broke out in your hometown.

- *Imagine, how might the decisions you made influence the lives of others—short term and long term?*

- *Imagine, how might the many decisions others have made in this hour influence your life, work, or family at some later time?*

Appreciative Leadership calls you to be conscious about your decisions, to be aware of when they align with your values and when they do not. Of special importance is the consistency of your decisions over time. Nothing stirs criticism in an organization more than inconsistency. And nothing generates respect more than the integrity that comes from open and timely communication, transparency, and opportunity for dialogue. The following stories show what can happen when conscious decision making is present and when it is not. Each of them ended differently than expected. The first shows how conscious decision making can put people at ease even in a challenging situation such as a layoff. The second shows how lack of integrity, in the form of inconsistency with espoused values, can quickly ramp up an organization's rumor mill in a negative and divisive way.

Story 1: As a way of building trust in leadership, the new general manager decided to engage all 1,200 employees from three shifts in a series of Appreciative Inquiry Summits. The purpose was to articulate strengths, principles, and priorities for strengthening their "hometown customer experience." The process was successful. Employees and customers were both enjoying the new culture of appreciation that was emerging. The process took place over three months. During that time the new general manager discovered that the CFO he had inherited when he took the job was misdirecting funds. The CFO was immediately removed from the position.

An immediate financial review made it clear that layoffs were inevitable. The general manager called us and asked, "How can we have an appreciative layoff?" He explained the situation. We spent several hours with him and his team, consciously considering the question. Ultimately we succeeded. Here are some of the things that happened:

- Managers were briefed about the situation and given coaching to brief their departments that afternoon, so that everyone would hear the news at the same time.
- The following two days, the general manager visited every department and every shift to listen and to answer questions.

- People were given choices including educational sabbaticals, job sharing, and early retirement.
- Everyone who was asked to leave was offered help with résumé writing and career counseling.
- A job fair was held on site.
- Two weeks following the layoffs, a series of two-hour Appreciative Inquiry meetings were held so people could grieve and discuss what happened.

The impact was surprisingly positive. The career counselor commented that of the 108 people whose jobs were eliminated, there were only 3 upset and angry people. It was the most positive layoff in his 20 years of experience! Six months later we were back working with one department. When we asked members of the department to describe the leadership team's strengths, they said integrity, approachability, and commitment.

Story 2: The leadership team said it was committed to Appreciative Inquiry, employee engagement, and collaboration. People got excited and began reaching out to each other in new ways. The seeds of change were planted, and then two new executives were hired. Both quickly gained a reputation for being top-down authoritarian leaders, rather than high-engagement appreciative leaders. Within weeks a year's worth of work was called into question. The grapevine was buzzing, "Why did they hire those kinds of people if they were really serious about employee engagement and collaboration?" "They don't really mean what they are saying. If they did, they would not have hired these guys." "I don't trust what they are saying. What they are doing just doesn't jive." " I thought things were going to change. Now I see that they are not."

Conscious decision making is a powerful practice for insuring integrity. Appreciative Leadership takes time to reflect, to talk with people, and to consider options in order to make decisions that are good for the whole. Some people have the luxury of unconscious decision making. Good things unfold without their conscious choice. They have safe places to live and they have enough food, they have work and colleagues who are meaningful to them, and they have loving friends and family. Unconscious decision making, however, is a luxury that most people in the world do not have. And it is a luxury that we must forgo in service to sustainability. Appreciative Leadership consciously attends to the choices they make, both personally and collectively to create a world that works for all.

Review your recent decisions. To what extent have they been relationship enhancing? Do they support the dignity and wholeness of all people and groups? Have you been conscious about how you generate and use resources like time and money? How have your decisions contributed to a world that works for all?

Empowering Principled Performance

Principled performance, be it personal or collective, draws upon strengths, in alignment with shared principles. Appreciative Leadership demonstrates integrity by engaging in principled performance, and empowering others to do the same.

All manner of performance—decision making, customer service, communication, collaboration, quality, and recognition—is guided by principles. Principles are the standards, beliefs, or codes of conduct that define appropriate and inappropriate performance. They often come to us in the form of folk wisdom: "You catch more flies with honey than vinegar." "A penny saved is a penny earned." "It takes two to tango."

Principles provide guidance about how to succeed; and as such, they serve as criteria for learning, assessment, and recognition. For example, the belief that you catch more flies with honey than vinegar suggests the need to *teach* people how to be kind, considerate, and sweet like honey; *assess* people to see how well they perform to the principle; and *recognize* people who successfully conduct themselves according to the principle and get the promised results, thereby catching more flies!

Reflect now on the principles that are most important to you and your success? Consider the following:

- What do you believe creates high performance?
- What do you believe is the appropriate role of supervision and management?
- What do you think contributes to learning, growth, and human development?
- What, for you, constitutes healthy relationships?
- What do you believe makes a great team?
- What is your code of conduct in relation to the natural environment?
- What are your standards of excellence?

As you can see, your principles are, a composite of your values and beliefs about the best way of being, working, learning, and living. They are statements of your ideals and as such they articulate your preferred leadership style and explain your performance. When your principles, your communication, and your performance are congruent, you are on the path of integrity. People will describe you as "walking the talk," and they will respect you and your expressions of leadership.

Appreciative Leadership empowers others to principled performance by helping them articulate and act on principles. This may be done by gathering people to discuss questions like those listed above; sharing and analyzing high-point stories for principles of success; or on-the-job coaching. To feel good about themselves, people must also feel good about what they do, the quality of their work, and the people with whom they work.

Sometimes people need to hear "well done" based on their principles. Other times they need coaching, to identify their principles and work to their own highest standards of excellence. Liz's story illustrates this:

She was having old tile floors in her home replaced with beautiful hardwood. By all standards, the team installing the new floor was doing a great job. And then they got to the kitchen. As they pulled out the refrigerator one last time to level it, they created visible scratches on the new floor. Sounds of frustration echoed through the house. Everyone huddled over the scratches. Could they be sanded out? Are they really noticeable? Should the scratched planks be replaced? The supervisor on the job said, "Liz, it's your floor. It is up to you. What would you like us to do?"

Liz thought about her own work principles for a while, and then she spoke to the two young installers: "I can live with the scratches. I am sure I will create even more over time. The real question is, can you? It's your decision. What do you need to do to have *pride in your work* when you finish this project?" The two looked at each other, smiled, and began pulling out the scratched planks. The next day as they finished and were leaving, one of the young men said to Liz, "I think this is the best floor I have ever done. Thanks for giving us the choice to do it right. It felt a lot better than being told what to do."

People have an implicit set of principles, a standard of excellence waiting to be called forth. Appreciative Leadership invites them to identify and to integrate their own personal principles by asking questions such as, "How will you know when you have done a good job?" or "What is your definition of success for this project, process, or procedure?" By inviting people to reflect on and articulate their own standards of excellence, appreciative leaders foster self-respect and accountability to quality and success. Telling people what to do builds fear of failure. Asking people to articulate and work to principles liberates energy, creates dedication to success, and fosters integrity at work. This is true for individuals and for teams.

Appreciative Leadership empowers principled performance in teams, departments, groups, and whole organizations by facilitating the discovery and articulation of *shared principles*. They use Appreciative Inquiry processes to engage with people to identify strengths, imagine the future, and then design a set of principles for working together.

Many medical schools today are engaging in curriculum redesign in order to stay relevant in light of changing expectations of students and society. The leadership of one notable school decided that curriculum redesign should take place in tandem with the design and construction of a new medical education building. They carried out a "holistic" design process using Appreciative Inquiry: the content of medical education, the pedagogy, and the space available were all simultaneously reinvented. The dedicated, exceedingly competent, and highly diverse group of faculty members responsible for the curriculum redesign were unable to coordinate their proposals until they created a set of shared principles. The time they invested in crafting their principles paid off. The principles made the job of assessing each other's work infinitely easier and much less conflictual. Their shared principles served as a framework for aligning their proposals and as criteria for determining final curriculum designs.

There are shared principles—collective wisdom about how to work together for the good of the whole—waiting to be accessed within all groups. It just needs to be discovered, articulated, and used as a foundation for collaboration.

Integrity: The Ultimate Measure of Organizational Success

Appreciative Leadership creates the conditions for sustainable high performance by engaging with others to articulate a set of shared principles. Once principles are articulated and agreed on, they become the way work is done and the measure of success. When you compliment someone on a job well done and he or she responds with "Thank you for noticing, that's how we do it around here," you know you have met someone working from shared principles.

Appreciative Leadership taps the well of positive power through principled performance. It assumes that people generally want to contribute their best to make a positive difference. It recognizes that, in order to succeed, people need to know what is expected of them and how to best apply their strengths.

As Figure 7-1 shows, principled performance occurs when people share a set of principles. The fulfillment of which invites them to apply their strengths.

It's a simple and powerful formula for creating high performance. The key to organizational success, however, is in ensuring that you have the right ingredients to accomplish your goals. Since your principles become your measure of success, it is absolutely and strategically essential that they be congruent with your mission, strategy, and goals. Successful organizations, businesses, schools, airlines, health care systems, and associations are principled in ways that support their mission and strategy.

As Figure 7-2 shows, success has two important measures: the degree to which your principles are integral to your mission, strategy, and goals; and the degree to which you live and work to your principles. In essence, integrity—the degree to which your mission,

FIGURE 7-1

A FORMULA FOR PRINCIPLED PERFORMANCE

Shared Principles	+	Applied Strengths	=	Principled Performance

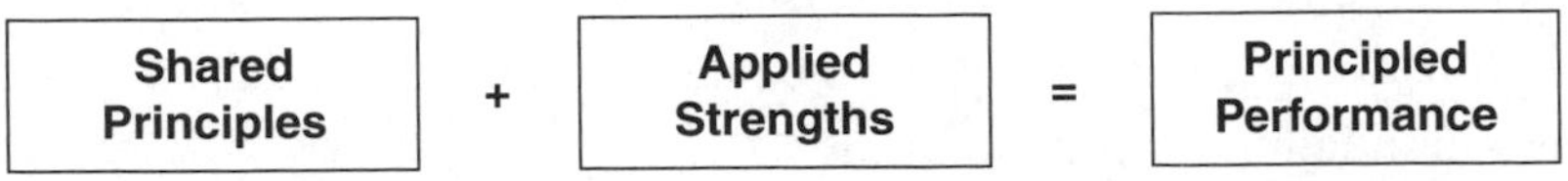

FIGURE 7-2

KEY INGREDIENTS OF ORGANIZATIONAL SUCCESS

strategy, principles, and strengths are in harmony—is the ultimate measure of organizational success. Following are three examples of highly principled organizations.

First is Rotary International. Its Four-Way Test of its core principles has been translated into over 100 languages. Rotarians around the world are united in asking themselves the same four questions in relation to what they think, say, or do:

1. Is it the Truth?
2. Is it Fair to all concerned?
3. Will it build Goodwill and Better Friendships?
4. Will it be Beneficial to all concerned?

Second is Green Mountain Coffee Roasters—a specialty coffee manufacturer based in Waterbury, Vermont—is driven by its core principle of World Benefit: "We are a force for good in the world. We celebrate and support the power of businesses and individuals to bring about positive changes, locally and globally." Company leaders live this principle by allocating 5 percent of the organization's pretax earnings to social and environmental causes. More importantly, they provide financial grants and support to local coffee growers and nongovernmental organizations (NGOs) around the world to help growers implement agricultural best practices, care for their health, diversify their income, and cultivate entrepreneurial skills—thereby building community across ethnic groups and helping to stabilize local economies in developing countries.

Finally, among the most principled organizations we know, the United Religions Initiative, was chartered in the year 2000 with a preamble, purpose, and set of principles to guide future decisions and growth. Now, ten years later, over 450 cooperation circles around the world have organized to carry out interfaith peace-building activities in alignment with their shared preamble, purpose, and principles.

So what does integrity cost? Not much compared to the lack of integrity, which will cost your success. It begins small. Without shared principles, good people do good work, but all in their own way. This creates lack of congruity, consistency, and standardization, all of which cost time, energy, and often money. And it magnifies: frustration grows, people distrust and blame each other, work and sometimes customers fall through the cracks. The costs of rework, customer dissatisfaction, and poor quality begin to mount. It gets your attention, and you begin losing sleep. Morale is at an all-time low; conflict is at an all-time high. The best people are leaving. People are not thriving at work; your health and that of others begins to suffer. Without shared principles, people do not hold together or work collaboratively. It shows, customers feel it, and they go elsewhere. As this scenario shows, lack of integrity creates a downward spiral of performance. And it keeps going down until you decide to turn it around.

Just as strategy must change to keep you current or ahead of industry and societal trends, so too must principles change. They must be reviewed and adapted whenever you change directions and strategies. And they must be reinvented to stay in sync with the changing demographics, values, and countenance of your workforce.

To Thine Own Self Be True

Appreciative Leadership embodies self-love. Integrity is a relational process requiring self-awareness and other awareness, self-care and other care, self-satisfaction and other satisfaction. To know what is important to yourself, and to be open and able to respond to what is important to other people—staff, customers, government agencies, even competitors, for example—is an essential Appreciative Leadership practice. Your integrity—your wholeness—reflects your personal preferences, your understanding of what other people need and want, and your ability to act in ways that honor it all. Whether a person, a team, or a whole department, Appreciative Leadership is true to itself, while caring for and meeting the needs of others—while working in service to the whole.

Moments before the start of the 50-meter freestyle semifinal at the Beijing Olympic Games, millions of people watched in surprise as U.S. swimmer Dara Torres rushed across the pool deck frantically waving her arms at poolside officials. When she reached the nearest official, the two spoke briefly and the competition was halted. Spectators later found out that a competitor from Sweden had torn her swimsuit, and Dara had asked the official to delay the race to allow for a quick suit change. Such gestures are rare. Dara enabled a competitor to stay in the race. She put aside her need to focus on a solid start off the block, putting her own performance in jeopardy—all because she believed in fair competition.

"To thine own self be true" is a saying that means many different things. The people we interviewed described being true to themselves as making decisions by trusting their intuition (their gut); acting in alignment with their values, principles, or beliefs; and working from their strengths and passions. They emphasized "doing what you believe is right, no matter what other people think" and "walking the talk." One younger colleague commented, it is "making sure that your audio and video are in sync."

In our experience, Appreciative Leadership practices include being true to yourself in seven important ways. All seven of these practices, summarized in Table 7-1, are required to unleash the positive power of integrity. The absence of any one of them will have negative consequences and derail you from the path of integrity.

TABLE 7-1 SEVEN PRACTICES FOR BEING TRUE TO YOURSELF
1. Do what you love, with people you respect.
2. Follow your dreams.
3. Work to your strengths.
4. Express your creative spirit.
5. Make value-based decisions.
6. Keep your word.
7. Be relationally responsible.

Do What You Love, With People You Respect

Being true to yourself means knowing who and what makes you happy, who and what gives you joy, and who and what brings out your best. Music legend Tina Turner asked, "What's love got to do with it?" When it comes to leadership, the answer is, "Everything." The path of integrity is a path of love. When you love your work and the people with whom you work, it shows. This is true for every kind of work in the world. When we say that someone is a "master" or "masterful," we mean that they do what they do with love. A master builder loves the process of design, loves the materials, and loves standing back in awe of the final result. A master teacher loves her students, loves life, and loves the subjects of her teaching. She takes joy in the process of human development. A master engineer once told us, "You just don't understand: We engineers who love what we do actually think we can build a better world than God!"

 Think about people you consider masterful:

- How do they demonstrate their love for what they do?
- How do they treat the people with whom they work?
- How do they demonstrate their care for people and resources?
- What do you most appreciate about them?

Follow Your Dreams

Know where you want to go and with whom. Focus your attention and resources to get there. Appreciative Leadership focuses on the future. On a personal level, Appreciative Leadership creates powerfully positive images in the form of aspirations and goals and works to realize them. It is disciplined, able to focus on strengths and transcend distractions to stay on the path of integrity. On a global level, Appreciative Leadership ensures that today's decisions, actions, and resources are mindfully used to support the well-being of generations to come. Johan Schaberg, editor of *Ode Magazine* in the Netherlands, has said it this way:

> The true leader doesn't set out to lead at all. Whether other people follow is, to him or her personally, of secondary importance. These kinds of leaders don't lead; they follow—a dream, an ideal, freedom for their country, a good life for their family. And they're very clear about it, which touches the people around them who then want to share in the dream. True, authentic leaders know they are connected to something bigger. Their wish is to serve that.[7]

Work To Your Strengths

Know your strengths—but also, value them and use them. When you truly appreciate your strengths and work from them, you make your life easier, you get better results, and you have more fun at work. In addition, others find it easier and more fun to work with you. Forcing yourself to do something that is not your strong suit creates frustration. It takes time in rework, and it lowers productivity. If you cannot describe your strengths or if you are not currently working to your strengths, it is time to renegotiate your job and/or talk to your human resources department or a career counselor for help in getting yourself back on track. Appreciative Leadership is strengths based. Your integrity depends on your knowing, appreciating, and working to your strengths.

Express Your Creative Spirit

Creative self-expression is a crucial part of being true to oneself. Let people know what you think, feel, and believe—what is important to you. In other words, express your creative spirit in ways that are natural and energizing to you, that reflect self-love, and are appropriate to the time and the situation. Self-expression that leaves other people feeling criticized or that blocks their well-intended efforts is not on the path of integrity. It is important to balance your need for self-expression with the needs of the people with whom you work. Your integrity depends on your capacity for "emotional intelligence."[8]

When we met Sue Ann she was a manager with big ideas and a big voice. She was powerful—just not positively so—because she interrupted people, talked longer and louder than anyone, and imposed her ideas on a regular basis. She didn't realize how inappropriate her style of communication was until she was denied a promotion for the third time. She asked for coaching. It was simple: She needed to learn to be positively powerful. She needed to learn to demonstrate the one thing she felt she never received: listening. It took a few months of studying other managers' communication styles and replicating the best, but she did it. She learned to sincerely listen and then to express her creative and generally very relevant ideas. The payoff was a new job in a new company in a city where she had always dreamed of living.

Make Value-Based Decisions

Align your decisions with what you tell people is important to you. In other words, make conscious decisions based on your values. Mark shared this story about how his wife lives her values and beliefs:

> My wife is a physical therapist and a Pilates instructor. She can make more money doing physical therapy, but she believes that Pilates is often much better for people. She will often tell clients that they don't need physical therapy and instead she'll recommend Pilates. It costs the client much less, and their results are much better. Although my wife gets less income, she wouldn't consider doing anything else. Her core beliefs and integrity shine through.

Appreciative leaders take time to gather people to clarify shared values, principles, and core beliefs. They consciously align all that they say and do with them. On a personal level, they use their values, principles, and beliefs as criteria for decisions and conduct. On an organizational level, they design values into all aspects of processes, systems, and structures. Many leadership teams say they value people; but few take the time to design this value into their management processes. When they do, the benefits are significant, as one tristate construction company in the Midwest discovered. The leadership team declared an end to terminations, layoffs, and firings. All processes that involved people separating from the company were redesigned and renamed "nurturing out processes." Resignations, retirements, layoffs, and terminations all became opportunities to "nurture out." The benefits: fewer legal disputes and increased productivity on the part of those who remained.

Keep Your Word

One of the simplest and clearest ways to demonstrate self-love is by keeping your word, your agreements, your promises, and your commitments. When you do, you will feel good about yourself, and others will feel good about you. Keeping your word generates self-respect as well as respect from others. You know the difference in these two scenarios:

- A supplier gives you an estimate for materials and tells you when they will arrive. Based on that information, you tell your customers when they can expect your final products. All is well until the supplier calls and says the order will be late. You call your customers, apologize, and set a new product delivery date. The materials come in, and you get the final products to your customers who pay for a job well done. Then you get the invoice from your supplier. It is higher than initially agreed upon. You decide to "cover the extra costs" yourself to preserve your customer relationship. The supplier loses you as a customer.

- A customer calls and needs a supply of materials within two days. She acknowledges that it is a last-minute order and asks if you can help. You say yes and then call your department together to figure out how to deliver on the promise you made. Good ideas fly around the room, people commit to working overtime, and one person even offers to hand-deliver the order if needed. Your team pulls together. Your customer gets what she needs when she needs it. You and your team feel pride in a job well done and gain self-respect.

Make agreements based on what is important to you, and keep them. The saying "A man is only as good as his word" applies to women as well. When you say you will do something, you are putting your identity on the line. Your identity, your integrity, and your self-respect all grow from keeping your word.

Be Relationally Responsible

Finally, when anything changes about what is important to you, or in your ability to do what you said you would do, immediately talk about it with the other people who are involved. The following story shows how one group of military leaders consciously chose to demonstrate relational responsibility:

Military protocol requires that enlisted personnel salute officers. A naval base commander noticed during his daily walk on a heavily trafficked pathway that many enlisted personnel were disregarding this protocol. The commander called his junior officers together to ask their opinions about how to address the situation. They came up with three options: (1) they could publicly "dress down" the enlisted personnel on the spot every time it happened; (2) they could ignore the breach of protocol; or (3) the officers could initiate the salute. They chose the last option. The next day the officers made a point to salute approaching enlisted personnel on the walkway. They received surprised looks and instant return salutes. In a matter of days, protocol was restored.

The people we interviewed stressed the significance of integrity. One person said emphatically, "When integrity is present, everything else falls into place. When it's not, you might as well stop right there." Being true to yourself is at the heart of being an appreciative leader.

 Recall a time when you were true to yourself: What was the situation? Who else was involved? What did you do to be true to yourself? How did it feel? What can you learn from this situation to be even more fully true to yourself in the future?

Right Relationships: A Hallmark of Appreciative Leadership

Being on the path of integrity takes work and constant attention. Think about trying to roll a boulder up a hill. It is hard work, and you must constantly be present lest your boulder roll backward. So it is with integrity. You cannot fall asleep on the path of integrity. It takes awareness and attention to the quality and propriety of your relationships to stay on the path.

Appreciative Leadership willingly and consciously considers and communicates with others about the many paradoxes of right relationship:

- To have respect for authority yet speak truth to power
- To give voice to youth yet harvest the wisdom of experience
- To honor equality yet recognize excellence
- To respect elders yet be open to fresh ideas
- To speak well of others yet be honest about abuse and violence

- To help those in need yet empower independence
- To honor cultural differences yet create shared meaning

This list could go on. Relationships are at the heart of our identities, our sense of community, and our ways of working. We live in an implicitly interconnected world. Relatedness is a given that can be strengthened or weakened by the way we communicate and interact with others and all living beings. Appreciative leaders nurture the bonds of relatedness by acting appropriately to the time and situation. They are students of humanity, open to learning about and accepting other people's ways of working and living. They believe in the essential goodness of all people, and they are willing to relate to them in ways that generate joy, happiness, and well-being for all.

One of the easiest ways to step off the path of integrity is to do something relationally inappropriate. It might be accidental yet based on habitual assumptions, such as calling a male nurse "Doctor" or the female physician "Nurse." Or it might be something unconscious or fear-based, such as hiring someone not suited for a job to ensure that you have no competition. It might even be something blatantly inappropriate such as yelling at people or criticizing them for not meeting expectations that you failed to communicate.

Remember: When you are off the path of integrity, it does not matter how you got off. What matters is how graciously and aptly you get back on.

Apologies help; and so does forgiveness. To say that you are sorry for unintended consequences of your decisions and actions does not mean that you were wrong. It means that you have the strength of character to help restore wholeness to someone else or some other group. For example, when Alex expressed concern over a series of business decisions his partner, Catherine, had made without involving him, she immediately recognized her oversight, apologized, and asked for ways that she could make things right. Having both shared his concern and been genuinely heard and acknowledged, Alex promptly forgave her.

To forgive other people or groups for their relational impropri-
eties that troubled or caused you problems does not make you weak.
It makes you a positively powerful leader able to bring out the best of
people and situations. Both apologies and forgiveness are practices
that help clear the air, set the record straight, and restore harmony in
a relationship.

There is a Taoist saying that we find especially useful in maintain-
ing right relationship. It suggests that "when we find something we
respect and admire about another person, we should make it our own.
And if there is something that troubles us about another person, we
should change it in ourselves."[9] The first part of this saying may come
easier to you—to learn from and adopt as your own that which you
value and respect about other people. The second part may be more
challenging to understand and to practice. If you are absolutely con-
vinced that someone else has a weakness, the last thing you want to
do is to admit to yourself that you too might have a variation of the
same weakness.

Take this example: Dick was always late for work, and when he
showed up, he wasted more time with excuses and reasons why he
was late. His colleague Shirley was frustrated. She continually blamed
Dick for their work being late: after all, he was the one who was late all
the time. When she finally took time for reflection, she realized that
she too had an issue with being late. And that she was conveniently
able to blame Dick for her own weakness. When she realized this, she
decided to get her work in on time, even if it meant doing so without
Dick's input. Surprisingly, as she started to get work done on time,
Dick started to show up on time in order to contribute and work with
her—which he truly enjoyed!

Determining what is relationally appropriate and what is inappropriate may not be easy. Often, the best that you can do is to consider
the options with an open mind and an open heart, talk to others who
are involved, and then determine what you believe is the most respectful course of action. Consider, for example, the relational complexities
in the following situation. How would you have handled it?

Carol is a VP who reports directly to the CEO. Audrey is an internal consultant working with both the CEO and his three peers in other business units. Carol and Audrey were having a monthly meeting to keep each other informed, when Carol offered the following advice: "People are saying that there is something wrong with James [business unit CEO]. I don't think he will be able to do the interviews you asked him to do without help. Would it be possible for you to offer him an assistant for the process, someone to take notes for him and be sure the right ideas get factored in?" Audrey thanked Carol for the input, and she said she would talk it over with colleagues and then get back to Carol with what was decided.

Audrey and her two colleagues discussed the situation. Was it really Carol's place to say that James needed help? What if he really did need help? What if James had a serious emotional or health issue? Should someone talk to James? If so, who? Should someone let James know what people were saying? Was it Audrey's place to find a way to provide help to James when he didn't ask for it?

After talking about the situation and considering a number of options, Audrey and her colleagues based their decision on the notion that *it is not appropriate to say something about someone that you have not said or are not willing to say to that person, directly.* They decided that Audrey would get back to Carol and tell her that if James asked for help, they would be happy to provide it. Otherwise, they felt they would be acting inappropriately and jumping into someone's life without being invited.

As this story makes apparent, the quality of relationships is an essential factor in the quality of performance. Determining what is relationally appropriate takes time, consideration, and care. And it is worth it. Right relationships are joyful sources of positive power, intimacy, learning, collaboration, and productivity. Appreciative Leadership fosters integrity through right relationships within departments and organizations, with customers and vendors, and across cultures, ages, and interests, as well as across business and community lines.

Honesty Is the Best Policy

Honesty is more than simply saying what's on your mind. It is about holding fast to that which is good—all the while lovingly but directly clearing away obstructions to that goodness. Why is honesty important? It gives us a sense of wholeness, and it stimulates the free flow of ideas and information. Dishonesty, by contrast, creates confusion, guilt, and shame. It blocks connection and creativity, and it even compromises our health.

Think about a time when you've shared your thoughts and feelings openly and completely, but kindly—perhaps even despite perceived obstacles or concerns. Most likely, that experience has been accompanied by a sense of relief and insight—perhaps even joy. Amy described a time like this, when she told the truth to a former boss:

> I had worked for him for only six months, but it had been the worst six months of my career. Throughout our time together I had felt questioned, criticized, and threatened. When he was promoted and left, I at first felt relief; then my resentment started to grow. Every time I'd see him, I'd feel angry and uncooperative—even vengeful.
>
> This was no way to live! Despite concerns that he might somehow retaliate, I decided to tell the truth. I met with him privately and directly shared my experience. I began by telling him that working for him had been terribly difficult but that it had taught me to look to myself for affirmation, rather than to my boss. The words had barely left my mouth when he interrupted me. "Oh boy," I thought, "this is it!"
>
> "Wait a minute," he said. "You thought I was criticizing you because I thought you weren't good? That couldn't have been further from the truth! You're one of the best employees I've ever had; and it frustrated me that you weren't living up to your full potential."

Needless to say, I was stunned. And though I deeply dis-
agreed with how he handled himself, I was *incredibly grateful*
to know the truth—as was he. He took my feedback to heart,
and started moderating his behavior around other employees.
Eventually, we became friends, staying connected with one
another years after we both left the company. All this happened because I took the risk to tell the truth.

It's easy to be honest when everything is going right. Though we
often forget to do so, it feels good to share our thoughts, feelings, and
ideas when we feel happy, fulfilled, respected, and safe. This suggests that
as we create nurturing and safe environments by practicing Appreciative Leadership, we encourage people to be honest with themselves, with
one another, and with us. Sheryl told us this story about what happened
when she received honest feedback from her workforce:

One day, a staff member came to my office, and said, "We've
got a problem. All of us got together and determined that we
can't work as fast as you, that we can't work your same long
hours. In other words, we can't be you. You have to lighten up
a little." I gave her a big hug and said, "I could have gone on
forever and not have known this. Thank you for telling me.
From now on, you say the word and I'll back off." Even though
it was difficult to hear, I kept my promise to listen to their
concerns, and our new way of operating worked really well.

Loving and supportive parents regularly share this kind of experience. When they create a sense of safety and support, their children are
more likely to "come clean" with mistakes. Or they will stay close to their
parents, even as they reject a family tradition or choose different values

from those by which they were raised. Take the son of the brigadier general who becomes a conscientious objector, the daughter of an evangelical Christian who becomes Muslim, the son of a conservative politician who announces he's gay, or the daughter of a feminist who chooses to be a stay-at-home mother. Choices to be true to ourselves—to be scrupulously honest, despite the consequences—are easier to make when we feel safe, secure, and supported.

Honesty is not just about what you say and do. It's also about what you *don't* say and do. Lies of omission, as they are called, can be just as damaging as those that are more direct. Take the leader who chooses to avoid telling a coworker that her behavior makes it hard for him to share his opinions. He is preventing her from seeing or understanding her impact on others, perhaps predisposing her for failure in the organization.

Let's face it: honesty may be the best policy, but it is often not the easiest one. To be honest with others, we first need to be honest with ourselves. This may mean facing up to something that is painful, scary, or even threatening. But courageous honesty with ourselves helps us see fully what is true; and from there, we can choose the path of goodness—of integrity. Human history is filled with stories of people who have chosen to step on the path of integrity. Being honest with themselves, they *said no* to corruption or oppression, choosing instead to preserve or protect a people or tradition, or to work in service of the greater good.

 Challenge yourself to even greater honesty over the next few days. Practice by starting your sentences with the word *honestly*. For example, "Honestly, the job I really want is …" "Honestly, the way I feel about this situation is …" "Honestly, what I think we need to do is …" Try it and see how it feels. Does what you are saying feel right in your gut? Do you believe what you are saying? Watch how others respond. Are they surprised? Do they value what you have to say?

Making the Most of Mistakes

The English poet Alexander Pope said, "To err is human." Rather than blaming and shaming people for making mistakes, appreciative leaders creatively turn errors into opportunities. They may do this by regarding mistakes as opportunities for learning; but when they are best, appreciative leaders intuitively follow one of the cardinal rules of improvisational theater, which is to say *"yes and ..."*—even to mistakes.

Consultant Frank Barrett quotes jazz trumpeter, bandleader, and composer Miles Davis as having said, "If you're not making a mistake, it's a mistake." He goes on to tell the story of how, in the middle of a recording session, one of Davis's band members played a blatantly wrong note. Davis promptly repeated the note—first once, then again—changing scales and building a whole new riff off of it. The result was an innovative, groundbreaking sound that sold hundreds of thousands of albums and continues to be emulated today.[10]

Appreciative Leadership turns honest mistakes into creative opportunities that demonstrate integrity and gain respect.

> In front of hundreds of people at a foundation gathering, I gave a grant recipient a wrong check. It was more money than we had planned to give the recipient. The vice president in charge of the event saw it as an opportunity. Rather than blame me and take the check back, apologize, and create a big drama, she turned it into a positive opportunity. After the event, she sent out an additional news release highlighting the award. The result was a large article in the local newspaper that led to more donations. Because she thought positively, we ended up benefiting from my mistake.

As this story illustrates, mistakes can lead to innovation. A safety manager at Boeing Corporation is quoted as having said, "When we have a failure, we try to replicate it. We repeat it to learn from it. We take this error, and we see what new information it can generate. It helps us see in new ways." Popular wisdom tells that 3M Post-it notes were invented from a bad batch of glue. Indeed, the theory of evolution itself shows how adaptive "mistakes" create new life forms. Learning from the best, Appreciative Leadership makes the most of mistakes.

Accounting for the Triple Bottom Line

From the beginning, Howard Schultz founder and chairman of Starbucks—described his founding impulse as more than money. He wanted to build a company with a conscience and consciously sought others with a similar dream. Tied together by their shared values and dreams, the Starbucks team continually seeks to achieve the fragile balance between profitability, shareholder value, a sense of benevolence, and a social conscience.

A 50-year-old mining company, Bord Na Móna, is Ireland's leading environmentally responsible, integrated utility service provider of electricity, heating, resource recovery, water, growing media, and related services. After engaging in an Appreciative Inquiry planning process, Bord Na Móna stakeholders adopted "A New Contract with Nature" that would move the company out of mining into a new world of renewable and environmentally friendly energy and recycling projects, along with conservation, planning, and development of its peatlands based on sound ecological principles.[11]

A young and growing chain of fast-food restaurants, Chipotle Mexican Grill, has adopted a "Food with Integrity" program that leads them to serve more naturally raised meat than any other restaurant in the country, push for more sustainable practices in produce farming, and work with dairy suppliers to eliminate the use of added hormones from their operations. In a break with competitive practices, the company also provides health benefits, a 401(K) plan, and paid vacation time for its employees.

In a similar vein, Google—known best for its search engine software—is widely recognized for its employee perks and benefits. In addition, the company makes high-profile environmental efforts, including adopting a goal to be a carbon-neutral company. Its philanthropic arm, Google.org, was created to find ways to fight climate change, poverty, and emerging diseases.

What do all of these organizations and communities have in common? They are on the vanguard of valuing and accounting for the "triple bottom line—people, profit, and planet":[12]

> In practical terms, *triple bottom line accounting* means expanding the traditional reporting framework to take into account ecological and social performance in addition to financial performance. The concept of the Triple Bottom Line demands that a company's responsibility be to stakeholders rather than shareholders. In this case, "stakeholders" refers to anyone who is influenced, either directly or indirectly, by the actions of the firm. According to the stakeholder theory, the business entity should be used as a vehicle for coordinating stakeholder interests, instead of maximizing shareholder (owner) profit.[13]

By measuring performance according to this triple bottom line, organizations and communities institutionalize the concept of integrity: of creating a world that works for all. This is an ancient concept, poignantly articulated in the Great Law, or constitution, of the Iroquois Nation: "Look and listen for the welfare of the whole people, and have always in view not only the present but also the coming generations, even those whose faces are yet beneath the surface of the ground—the unborn of the future Nation."[14]

Operating from a stance of integrity—of consistent and conscious concern for the whole—appreciative leaders operate from a place of discernment. They take the long view, and they strive to make choices for the good of the whole, both now and in the future.

Enhancing Your Capacity:
Resources for Further Development

TABLE 7-2 INTEGRITY: A SUMMARY OF KEY PRACTICES		
	Key Practices	**Page Numbers**
Personal	• Engage in conscious decision making.	166
	• Be true to yourself.	176
One-to-one	• Empower principled performance.	170
	• Foster right relationship.	183
Team or group	• Measure success by your principles.	174
	• Make the most of mistakes.	190
Whole organization or community	• Work in service to the whole.	161
	• Account for the triple bottom line.	191

Recommended Books

Cannibals With Forks: The Triple Bottom Line of the 21st Century by John Elkington (Oxford: Capstone Publishing, Ltd.), 1997.

The Ecology of Commerce: A Declaration of Sustainability by Paul Hawken (New York: HarperCollins Publishers), 1993.

Edgewalkers: People and Organizations That Take Risks, Build Bridges, and Break New Ground by Judi Neal (Westport, CT: Praeger), 2006.

Emotional Intelligence by Daniel Goleman (New York: Bantam Books), 1995.

Recommended Web Sites

Center for Business as an Agent for World Benefit

http://worldbenefit.case.edu

The Center for Business as an Agent for World Benefit (BAWB) helps companies, entrepreneurs, and industry associations turn the world's social and ecological issues into bona fide business opportunities—uniting the strengths of markets with the challenge of achieving a sustainable earth.

Green Business

http://www.greenbusiness.net/triple-bottom-line.html

A discussion list by and for eco entrepreneurs and professionals who use triple bottom line practices to grow their businesses every day.

The Tyson Center

http://waltoncollege.uark.edu/news/view.asp?article=704

The mission of the Tyson Center is to advance the state of research, practice, and teaching in the field of faith and spirituality in the workplace. It is a resource center for business leaders, academics, spiritual and faith leaders, and practitioners.

EIGHT

Making a Positive Difference with Appreciative Leadership

Leadership makes things happen. Appreciative Leadership makes good things happen, and it does so in positive, life-affirming ways. It is a source of human well-being and a foundation for thriving organizations and communities. By employing the five strategies of Appreciative Leadership and the many practices presented in the prior chapters, you will make a positive difference—directly, in the lives of those you touch, and indirectly, for seven generations to come.[1] Your impact may be personal or systemic, social or financial, local or global. Ultimately they are all interrelated.

As you adopt and adapt the strategies and practices of Appreciative Leadership and make them your own, be guided by your strengths, interests, and areas of responsibility. Your strengths, interests, and responsibilities will coalesce in the area in which you can be most effective as an appreciative leader. They will indicate your unique domain of positive power. They will reveal the way in which you can be most powerful and make the most positive difference in the world.

Appreciative Leadership in Action

You can use Appreciative Leadership practices to meaningfully make a difference in the lives of others one at a time, or collectively through programs and policies, social innovation, collaboration, and transformation. Every day, people throughout the world make a positive difference in the lives of others.

Read this list of appreciative leaders slowly, as if poetry, through the lens of your appreciative eyes:

- People who say hello in the hallways, who hold doors open for young and old alike, who smile first or comment on a beautiful day
- Soldiers serving on behalf of peace, saying it is an honor to risk their lives to defend their country and protect their loved ones
- Artists painting, singing, and dancing beauty, harmony, and joy into life on canvas, television, and YouTube
- Researchers seeking cures and prevention for illnesses such as cancer, heart disease, Alzheimer's disease, and HIV/AIDS
- Students reading books, attending college, technical school, seminary, or medical school, studying to learn and enhance their abilities to contribute to society
- Parents fighting to overcome adversity, cold weather, illness, famine, immigration, or war to care for their families
- Women and men of spirit and religion who pray and conduct ceremonies for the well-being of others
- People who put aside historical injustice to forgive and heal the divides that separate people and societies
- Grandmothers and grandfathers who fill the hearts and minds of children with stories of hope for a better life
- Elected and volunteer public officials and workers who care for the infrastructures of our societies
- And, yes, CEOs of major corporations whose foresight and abilities to align complex social, political, environmental, and economic dynamics get cars on the streets, cereal on the breakfast tables, and medicines in the pharmacies

They are role models living and working in accord with their highest ideals and images of a better world. They are Appreciative Leadership in action, each and every one of them.

Being Appreciative Leadership: Oh, the Difference You Will Make

Mahatma Gandhi's famous directive to those who would change the world, "Be the change you wish to see," is especially relevant for those who would be appreciative leaders. By employing the strategies and practices of Appreciative Leadership, you will over time *become* Appreciative Leadership. As you don the mantle of Appreciative Leadership, you will make a positive difference. Figure 8-1 shows the relationship between Appreciative Leadership and positive results.

Cultivate Your Character

The first and most essential way you will make a positive difference is by cultivating your character. By practicing Appreciative Leadership, you will become a better person and leader of unquestionable integrity, able to work more consistently at your best. Each and every one of us has a seed of potential, an inherent positive core to be realized.

FIGURE 8-1

GETTING POSITIVE RESULTS WITH APPRECIATIVE LEADERSHIP

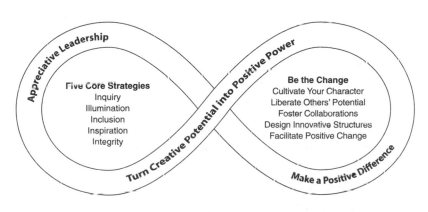

In some cultures children are named to reflect their potential. Family and community members listen to the spirit of the child before it is born to learn the gifts it is bringing to the world and to hear its name.[2] In other societies, young people are taken on as apprentices at an early age so that their implicit talents can be revealed. Everyone has potential; and everyone is responsible for its cultivation.

It may seem to you that your own personal development is a small contribution when compared to saving the rain forest, inventing a new technology, or managing a city. Personal development may seem small; but it is not. It is the first and most essential way to make a positive difference. It creates a solid foundation for organization and community life. The Lakota phrase *Lena ecunk'unpi, hecel oyate ki ninpe kte*[3] translates to say, "We do these things so the people may live." This means that everything we do has an impact on the life of the people. Everything. So whatever you do to develop your strengths, talents, knowledge, and wisdom makes a positive difference. Personal development in any of the following areas strengthens your capacity to make a positive difference in the lives of others:

- *Cultural awareness*: Recognize, respect, and communicate with people of differing cultures, lifestyles, and worldviews.
- *Emotional intelligence*: Appropriately sense and express emotions, and listen compassionately and respond to those expressed by others.
- *Appreciative intelligence*: See the inherent positive potential in a person or situation.
- *Technology friendliness*: Be at ease learning and using technology.
- *Physical well-being*: Make choices that promote physical fitness, strength, and health.
- *Financial savvy*: Earn, use, and give away money in ways that care for self, family, and society.
- *Environmental sensitivity*: Actively support human activities that respect and care for the earth and all living beings.

- *Spiritual intelligence:* See the world and oneself through a God- or spirit-centered lens, and adapt one's life and actions accordingly.

Cultivating your own character is then an important way in which you can make a positive difference in the world; but it is not necessarily easy. It takes courage, dedication, patience, and support to explore, learn about, and develop yourself. Practices to help you do this include recognizing and using your strengths, expanding your inner dialogue, and engaging in conscious decision making.

Liberate Others' Creative Potential

A second way in which you will make a positive difference through Appreciative Leadership is by liberating other people's creative potential. Appreciative Leadership holds all people in positive regard. Appreciative leaders are coaches and facilitators dedicated to helping others be the best they can be. They make a positive difference through strengths-based inquiry, dialogue, and communication; and they liberate the creativity of others and instill confidence by encouraging people to discover, express, and realize their strengths, hopes, and dreams.

People who work from their strengths, listen to their intuition, and follow their dreams are generally happier, healthier, and more productive than people who just work for the money. Any time you help people recognize their strengths and redefine their job to use their strengths, you are making a positive difference. Any time you listen to the intuition or the "crazy idea" of another person, you are opening the door for his or her creativity to flow. Any time you help individuals make choices that are good for them, that are healthy, or that improve the quality of their lives, you are making a positive difference in the world.

Take John as an example. A Web site designer by trade, John loves technology—a love that he eagerly shares with his clients. His transparent systems invite experimentation and play; and whenever asked, he actively educates and coaches. The effect? Even middle-aged technophobes gain courage and competence. John's inquisitive and affirming style brings out the best in others.

Appreciative Leadership holds life as central. It puts life at the heart of everything it does and says. Its most indispensable measure of success is this: To what extent do our actions nurture life? Feed people? Make people happy? Care for the planet? Spread the wealth? Bring out the best of people and situations? The people we have interviewed said that great leadership is "people centric." We believe this; but we also believe that in this day and age it is not sufficient to be merely people centric. While "liberating creative potential" generally refers to coaching, mentoring, supervising, managing, and leading—those actions that bring out the best of people—it also acknowledges leadership that cares for and brings out the best of all members of our living ecosystem. Appreciative Leadership is life centric in its care for the whole.

Whatever you do that builds confidence, enhances skills, inspires creativity, or expands someone's worldview makes a positive difference in the world. Practices such as strengths spotting and appreciative coaching will help you do just that.

Foster Collaboration across Divided Lines

A third and globally essential way you will make a positive difference by practicing Appreciative Leadership is by fostering collaboration across divided lines. When we interviewed people about what they wanted from leadership, the most frequent responses we received were these: collaboration, to be engaged with others at work, to be involved with others making decisions, and to cooperate with others in the creation of a shared future. People at all levels and functions of businesses, health care systems, schools, and communities believe that work goes better with collaboration.

Not only is collaboration what people want; according to evolutionary biologist Dr. Elisabet Sahtouris, a thought leader in the field of global well-being, it is what they need. She has written, "Our worldwide economic system, our transportation and communications technology, our information revolution, have bound us into a body of humanity that is now being pushed for the sake of its survival to evolve from competition to cooperation among people, among nations, and with our environment. ... I believe that we are capable of regaining our reverence for life, of replacing the drive to conquer with the will to cooperate."[4]

As you can see, fostering collaboration across divided lines holds great potential. The obvious place to start is within your own team, department, or group. The more impactful opportunities for collaboration, however, are across lines that exist among people who are in some way different or even in conflict. Appreciative Leadership makes a positive difference in the world by bringing improbable groups together, by building bridges of collaboration, and by joining with others to create a shared future.

By fostering collaboration across divided lines, Appreciative Leadership strengthens the relational fabric of organizations and communities, thereby creating new possibilities for action and impact. Practices such as appreciative check-ins and inviting improbable participation will help you to do this.

Design Innovative Social Structures

Perhaps the most enduring way your Appreciative Leadership can make a positive difference in the world is as you design innovative social structures. Appreciative Leadership creates a lasting legacy by designing values into the social structures that shape our lives. Winston Churchill said of the relationship between structures and performance, "First we design our structures, and then they design us." Recognizing the power of social structures to influence performance and the quality of life, Appreciative Leadership designs policies, programs, products, services, technology, and organizational cultures that are strengths based, life affirming, and appreciative.

You may think that you are not in a position to design new ways of doing things. Well, think again: leadership is about design—the design of meetings; the design of marketing campaigns; the design of products, services, and policies; the design of strategic plans and partnerships; even the design of markets, governance systems, economies, and currencies. The task of leadership is to design values into structures so they become living values and the inevitable ways of doing things.

Frances Perkins, sometimes described as "the woman behind the New Deal," dedicated her life to designing life-affirming structures. With her upper-middle-class values and education, she was an unlikely champion for the downtrodden and disadvantaged; yet from the beginning, she directed her tremendous intelligence, intuition, and political savvy to further progressive economic and social programs that today are considered commonplace. Eventually appointed secretary of labor under Franklin Delano Roosevelt (the first woman to hold a U.S. Cabinet-level position), she conceived of and shepherded into law some of the first minimum wage, industrial safety, and child labor laws in the country, the institution of the Social Security and Unemployment Insurance programs, and the establishment of the National Labor Relations Board. Despite inevitable public criticism and political attack, she continued to work tirelessly until her death to fulfill her dreams of America as an exemplar of justice, compassion, and opportunity for all.

In order to design innovative social structures, you must also cultivate your character, liberate other people's creative potential, and foster collaboration across divided lines. High-engagement practices presented throughout this book—such as the Appreciative Inquiry Summit and accounting for the triple bottom line—will help you do just this.

Facilitate Positive Change

Finally, by practicing Appreciative Leadership, you will make a positive difference as you facilitate positive change. Everything that Appreciative Leadership does focuses on positive change: from personal development to coaching to large-scale transformation. Appreciative leaders make a positive difference by using Appreciative Inquiry. AI is the leading process for effecting positive change at all levels of human interaction and organization; for strategic planning and culture transformation; for management development and executive team development; for union/management partnerships; and for building and community planning. Whitney and Trosten-Bloom's *The Power of*

Appreciative Inquiry has been described as the most practical and accessible book on the subject. We recommend it as a primer for making a positive difference in the world by facilitating positive change.

Be The Change

Now, today, the world is calling for Appreciative Leadership. You and others have answered the call. May all your thoughts, words, and actions make the kind of difference you have imagined. May you indeed be the change you wish to see in the world.

Conclusion

MAKE A CAREER OF HUMANITY.... YOU WILL MAKE A GREATER
PERSON OF YOURSELF, A GREATER NATION OF YOUR COUNTRY,
AND A FINER WORLD TO LIVE IN.
—MARTIN LUTHER KING, JR.

Appreciative Leadership exists at all levels and in all positions of an organization or community. It resides among people as a force for elevated performance and positive change. A relational dynamic, it emerges when people join together for a common cause, a meaningful purpose, or a provocative curiosity in ways that bring out the best of each other and the situation. At its best Appreciative Leadership is

- *Inquiry based:* Recognizing that people and groups move in the direction of what they study, Appreciative Leadership puts forth questions more often than prescriptions.
- *Illuminating:* Appreciative Leadership sees people and the world as they are—for better and for worse; and it chooses to live and work in the energetically positive, to bring out the best.
- *Inclusive, engaging, and inviting:* Appreciative Leadership extends its relational reach in order to ensure that everyone whose future it is has a voice in creating the future. It fosters inquiry and dialogue across divides and among improbable pairs.
- *Inspiring and life affirming:* Appreciative Leadership unleashes the creative spirit and gives hope for the future. In so doing, it mobilizes people's hearts, minds, and hands toward visions of a better world.
- *Integral and Holistic:* Appreciative Leadership holds forth *integrity.* It lives, works, and serves in support of human well-being, life-affirming organizations, and a sustainable world.

Appreciative Leadership is our hope for a better world. A growing force, it is not yet the norm in all organizations or communities around the world, but it has been fully embraced in many. We are fortunate to have worked with many such organizations and communities, and we have written about them in this book:

- Owners of the Brazilian food company who invited all employees, together with suppliers and community leaders, to cocreate the future of the business. That business is now a leading health food company.
- Leadership of a mining company in Ireland that reinvented itself as a force for global sustainability by designing "a new contract with nature."
- The new general manager of a hotel and casino who successfully led "appreciative downsizing."
- The executive team of a major health care system that committed to "moving as one into the future" on behalf of patient quality and service.
- The U.S. Anti-Doping Agency, which holds itself to the same high standards of excellence exhibited by athletes who fully embrace "true sport."
- Province leadership of the Sisters of the Good Shepherd who engaged over 650 people in a long-range direction-setting process, leading a 91-year-old Sister to comment, "You are never too old to contribute."
- The enlightened leaders of Green Mountain Coffee Roasters who ensure that growers and consumers all benefit from their coffee experience.
- Admirals of the U.S. Navy who hosted and participated in a series of 200-person summits to foster leadership at all levels throughout the Navy.

These leaders and the appreciative organizations they lead give us hope. They are exemplars of Appreciative Leadership. By mobilizing creative potential and turning it into positive power and performance, they are making a positive difference in the world and leaving a positive legacy.

Now It's Your Turn

 It is time for you to consider all that you have learned about yourself and Appreciative Leadership as you read this book. The following three pages provide guidance for you: to review what you have learned, to envision your future with Appreciative Leadership, and to write the story of your Appreciative Leadership legacy. Begin by noting:

- What new insights do you have about yourself as an appreciative leader?

- How would you describe your Appreciative Leadership strengths and capacities?

- With which of the Five Core Strategies—inquiry, illumination, inclusion, inspiration, or integrity—are you most comfortable?

- Which strategy or specific practice gives you the greatest sense of satisfaction?

- What ideas do you have for applying Appreciative Leadership? In other words, what project—large or small—might benefit from Appreciative Leadership?

- What specific Appreciative Leadership practice might add value to your department, team, or community?

- What aspect of Appreciative Leadership do you want to develop more fully in your life?

With all this as backdrop, it's time to look to the future. Imagine that it's five years from today. A new edition of *Appreciative Leadership*:

Focus on What Works to Drive Winning Performance and Build a Thriving Organization has just been pubished. Your Appreciative Leadership story is prominently featured. Consider and make note on the following questions:

- What are you doing now? With whom?

- How are you demonstrating Appreciative Leadership?

- Which of the Five Core Strategies is your greatest strength?

- How and with whom did you become proficient doing it?

- In what specific ways are you turning potential into positive power and performance on a regular basis?

- How are others responding and benefiting from your acts of Appreciative Leadership?

- What positive differences are you making? What legacy are you leaving for generations to come?

When you are done reflecting and making notes, *write your Appreciative Leadership Story* in the space that follows. Write it in the present tense ("I am") as an affirmation of who you are being.

Review it every three to six months, and watch it come to life. If you wish, e-mail a copy to appreciativeleadership.org, along with your name and contact information. With your permission, we will share it on our Web site, www.appreciativeleadershipnow.com.

My Appreciative Leadership Story

Our Vision for the Future of Appreciative Leadership

It only seems fair that we would share our story with you. Five years have passed. Another group of extraordinary women and men have just completed our Appreciative Leadership Development Program. In so doing, they join the ranks of thousands of people around the world who are practicing, experimenting with, and extending our initial understandings of Appreciative Leadership.

We are traveling around the world giving keynote speeches and teaching about Appreciative Leadership. Wherever we go, we hear story after story of people whose lives have been changed for the better as a result of Appreciative Leadership. Corporations on every continent have adopted the five strategies as a framework for building thriving organizations. Communities hold public officials, small businesses, and service providers accountable for the highest standards of Appreciative Leadership. And schools have designed relational curricula using Appreciative Leadership practices as their foundation. As a result, people, profits, and the planet are flourishing.

This is our vision. May it be so.

Endnotes

Introduction

1. Diana Whitney and Amanda Trosten-Bloom, *The Power of Appreciative Inquiry,* 2nd ed. (San Francisco: Berrett-Koehler, 2010), pp. 270–271.

2. From an interview conducted by Donna Havens, Ph.D., RN, FAAN, professor at the University of North Carolina at Chapel Hill, May 2007.

3. From an interview with Sister Mary Carolyn McQuaid of the Sisters of the Good Shepherd, Province of Mid-North America (PMNA), May 2007.

4. Shared anonymously in an interview with a corporate manager.

5. Shared by Sister Barbara Beasley of the Sisters of the Good Shepherd, Province of Mid-North America (PMNA), May 2007.

6. Shared anonymously in an interview with a community leader.

7. (Focus group participants generously agreed that we could share their comments and stories, but requested that we not share their names.

8. Paraphrased from words attributed to Mahatma Gandhi.

Chapter 1

1. R. S. Brutoco, President's Report Year 2002 in *Review: Year in Perspective 2002: Responsibility for the Whole* (Ojai, CA: World Business Academy, 2002), p. 9.

2. Kenneth J. Gergen, *Relational Being: Beyond Self and Community* (New York: Oxford University Press, 2009), p. 331.

3. Ibid.

4. Vuyisile Msila, Faculty of Education, Nelson Mandela Metropolitan University, *Ubuntu and School Leadership, Journal of Education,* no. 44, 2008.

5. M. Schiller, B. M. Holland, and D. Riley, editors, *Appreciative Leaders: In the Eye of the Beholder* (Chagrin Falls, OH: Taos Institute Publications, 2001), p. 158.

6. Ibid., p. 50.

7. http://www.washingtonpost.com/wp-dyn/content/article/2008/01/08/AR2008010804032.html, retrieved November 16, 2009.

8. Schiller, Holland, and Riley, p. xi.

Chapter 2

1. http://www.merriam-webster.com/, retrieved November 18, 2009.

2. Excerpted from Marianne Williamson, *A Return to Love: Reflections on the Principles of "A Course in Miracles"* (New York: HarperCollins, 1992).

Chapter 3

1. Diana Whitney and Amanda Trosten-Bloom, *The Power of Appreciative Inquiry,* 2nd ed. (San Francisco: Berrett-Koehler, 2010), pp. 66–67.

2. Tojo Thatchenkery and Carol Metzker, *Appreciative Intelligence: Seeing the Mighty Oak in the Acorn* (San Francisco: Berrett-Koehler, 2006), p. 5.

3. Ron Fry and Frank Barrett, "Rethinking What Gives Life to Positive Change," in *Appreciative Inquiry and Organizational Transformation: Reports from the Field*, edited by Ron Fry, Frank Barrett, Jane Seiling, and Diana Whitney (Westport, CT: Quorum, 2002), pp. 263–278.

4. Susan O. Wood, "Creating a Positive Future for Nursing Using Appreciative Inquiry," *AI Practitioner*, February 2004, pp. 13–18.

Chapter 4

1. Christopher Robert and Wan Yan, "The Case for Developing New Research on Humor and Culture in Organizations: Toward

a Higher Grade of Manure," in *Research in Personnel and Human Resources Management*, vol. 26 (Bingley: Emerald Publishing Group, 2007), pp. 205–267.

2. Susan O. Wood, "Creating a Positive Future for Nursing Using Appreciative Inquiry," *AI Practitioner*, February 2004, pp. 13–18.

3. Jennifer Fox, M.Ed., *Your Child's Strengths: Discover Them, Develop Them, Use Them* (New York: Penguin Group, 2008), pp. 126–128.

4. Barbara L. Fredrickson, *Positivity* (New York: Crown Publishers, 2009).

5. Marcial F. Losada and Emily Heaphy, "The Role of Positivity and Connectivity in the Performance of Business Teams: A Nonlinear Dynamics Model," *American Behavioral Scientist*, vol. 47, no. 6, 2004, pp. 740–765.

6. David L. Cooperrider and Diana Whitney, *Appreciative Inquiry: A Positive Revolution in Change* (San Francisco: Berrett-Koehler, 2005).

7. Jon M. Gotman and Nan Silver, *Seven Principles for Making Marriage Work* (New York: Three Rivers Press, 1999).

Chapter 5

1. Kenneth J. Gergen, *An Invitation to Social Construction* (London: Sage Publications, 2005, original edition 1999).

2. Kenneth J. Gergen and Mary Gergen, *Social Construction: An Invitation to the Dialogue* (Chagrin Falls, OH: Taos Institute Publications, 2004), p. 8.

3. Diana Whitney and Amanda Trosten-Bloom, *The Power of Appreciative Inquiry*, 2nd ed. (San Francisco: Berrett-Koehler, 2010), p. 193.

4. David L. Cooperrider, "The Child as Agent of Inquiry," *OD Practitioner*, vol. 28, 1996, pp. 5–11.

5. "Stories and Facts: The Talking Stick," by Carol Locust, Ph.D., http://www.acaciart.com/stories/archive6.html, retrieved February 1, 2010.

6. Endorsement for James D. Ludema, Diana Whitney, Bernard J. Mohr, and Thomas J. Griffin, *The Appreciative Inquiry Summit: A Practitioner's Guide for Leading Large-Group Change* (San Francisco: Berrett-Koehler, 2003).

Chapter 6

1. We give thanks to Howard Bad Hand, Lakota Holy Man, for the phrase "the energetically positive."

2. Adapted with gratitude from a story about Lubavitcher Rebbe written by Arnie Gotfryd in *Chabad Holiday Review*, vol. 18 (Albuquerque, NM, 2009).

3. Informal conversation with Tom White, president, GTE, Telecommunications Division.

4. Lev S. Vygotsky and Alex Kozulin, editors, *Thought and Language*, rev. ed. (Cambridge, MA: MIT Press, 1986).

5. Michael White, *Maps of Narrative Practice* (New York: Norton, 2007), p. 271.

6. Dr. Diana Whitney, president, Corporation for Positive Change, and Dr. Patricia Arenas, director, Human Change Project of the Center for Psychological and Sociological Research in Havana, Cuba, were the first recipient pair.

7. "Cultures of Participation at Work in Cuba and the United States," *OD Practitioner*, vol. 38, no. 4, 2006; and Arenas Bautista, P. y M. L. Monette, et al., editors, *Culturas de Participacion del Trabajo en Cuba y los Estados Unidos*, CIPS (Publicaciones Acuario Centro Felix Varela, 2007).

8. Book of Proverbs, 29:18.

9. Taken from a painting of the same name depicting a New England Bell lineman patrolling telephone lines in snowshoes during the Blizzard of 1888.

10. Diana Whitney and Amanda Trosten-Bloom, *The Power of Appreciative Inquiry*, 2nd ed. (San Francisco: Berrett-Koehler, 2010), pp. 250–255.

11. David L. Cooperrider, "Positive Image, Positive Action: The Affirmative Basis of Organizing" in *Appreciative Management and Leadership: The Power of Positive Thought and Action in Organizations*, edited by Suresh Srivastva and David L. Cooperrider (San Francisco: Jossey-Bass, 1990), pp. 91–125.

12. Jack Nicklaus, Jim McQueen (illustrator) with Ken Bowden, *Golf My Way*, rev. ed. (New York: Simon & Schuster, 2005).

13. Barbara L. Fredrickson, *Positivity* (New York: Crown, 2009), p. 43.

14. Fred Luthans and Bruce Avolio, "Authentic Leadership Development," in *Positive Organizational Scholarship*, ed. Kim S. Cameron, Jane E. Dutton, and Robert E. Quinn, 253 (San Francisco: Berrett-Koehler, 2003).

15. Antoine de Saint-Exupery and Richard Howard, translator, *The Little Prince* (Boston: Houghton Mifflin Harcourt, 2000), pp. 83–86.

16. Howard E. Butt, Jr., *The Stonemasons*, http://www.thchighcalling. org/Library/ViewMessage.asp?MessageID=24, retrieved November 19, 2009.

17. http://www.gmcr.com/about-GMCR.html, retrieved November 19, 2009.

18. Muhammad Yunus and Alan Jolis, *Banker to the Poor: Micro-Lending and the Battle Against World Poverty* (New York: PublicAffairs, 2003).

19. http://www.pbs.org/opb/thenewheroes/meet/ruiz.html, retrieved November 19, 2009

20. http://worldbenefit.case.edu/, retrieved November 19, 2009.

Chapter 7

1. Huston Smith and Jeffrey Paine, *Tales of Wonder* (New York: HarperCollins, 2009), p. 134.

2. Diana Whitney and David L. Cooperrider, "The Appreciative Inquiry Summit: An Emerging Methodology for Whole System Positive Change," *OD Practitioner*, vol. 32, 2000, pp. 13–26.

3. Joseph Jaworski, *Synchronicity: The Inner Path of Leadership* (San Francisco: Berrett-Koehler, 1996), p. 182.

4. Diana Whitney, "Appreciative Inquiry: Creating Spiritual Resonance in the Workplace," *Journal of Management, Spirituality and Religion*, publication pending.

5. Tyson Center for Faith and Spirituality, http://waltoncollege. uark. edu/news/view.asp?article=720, retrieved November 19, 2009.

6. Jimmy Carter, "Losing My Religion for Equality," in a letter written July 14, 2009, http://www.theage.com.au/opinion/losing-my-religion-for-equality–20090714-dk0v.html?page=-1, retrieved November 19, 2009.

7. Johan Schaberg, "Everyone Can Be a Leader," *Ode Magazine*, March, 2005, http://www.odemagazine.com/doc/21/everyone_can_be_a_leader, retrieved November 19, 2009.

8. Daniel Goleman, *Emotional Intelligence* (New York: Bantam Books, 1995).

9. Adapted from Richard Wilhelm and Cary F. Baynes, translators, *The I Ching, or Book of Changes*, 3rd ed. (Princeton, NJ: Princeton University Press, 1967).

10. Excerpted from a presentation by Frank Barrett, Ph.D., associate professor of systems management with the Naval Post-Graduate School, at the Second International Conference on Appreciative Inquiry, September 19–22, 2004.

11. Background information provided by Paul O'Kelly and Peter Hanan of O'KellySutton, http://www.okellysutton.ie/, retrieved November 19, 2009.

12. The phrase "triple bottom line" was coined by John Elkington in 1994. It was later expanded upon in John Elkington, *Cannibals with Forks: the Triple Bottom Line of 21st Century Business* (Mankato, MN: Capstone Publishing, 1997).

13. http://en.wikipedia.org/wiki/Triple_bottom_line, retrieved November 19, 2009.

14. http://www.indigenouspeople.net/iroqcon.htm, retrieved on November 7, 2009.

Chapter 8

1. We respectfully use the phrase "for seven generations" as it is currently used in popular culture, to mean having an impact on the future. For some Native American communities, however, it means seven generations backward and forward. The belief is that actions today impact what has happened in the past as well as what will happen in the future.

2. Sobonfu Some, *The Spirit of Intimacy: Ancient African Teachings in the Ways of Relationships* (New York: HarperCollins, 2000).

3. Translated by Howard Bad Hand, author, *Native American Healing* (New York: McGraw-Hill, 2001).

4. Elisabet Sahtouris, *Earthdance: Living Systems in Evolution* (Bloomington, IN: iUniverse, 2000).

Contributors of Story and Spirit

Writing, like leadership, is a relational process. There are many people with whom we have been in dialogue about the ideas in this book for a long time, some for as long as 30 years. There are others who have been role models and teachers helping us clarify our thinking and better live by the principles we espouse. And still others who have offered challenges that have served to strengthen our belief in an appreciative approach to leadership. This book could not have been written without them all. Thank you to all our relations, friends, family, colleagues, and clients. And to the people, organizations, and communities named below, we offer our deep and heartfelt appreciation for your stories, for your encouragement, and for all you have done to nurture the spirit of this book.

Jon Abels, John Adams, Marilee Adams, Harlene Anderson, Patricia Arenas, Tony Aucock, Rebecca Auman, Sr. Sharon Rose Authorson, Michel Avital, Emily and Dick Axelrod

Howard Bad Hand, Sr. Barbara Beasley, Ron Bell, Sarajo Berman, David Berry, Scott Blackmun, Norm Blake, Sabine Bredemeyer, Kim Brown, Mike Burns

Robert Caldwell, Michelle Carter, Paul Chaffee, Sam Chan, Dinesh Chandra, Louis Cocciolone, Stephan Cocciolone, David Cooperrider

Maura Da Cruz, Sean Daly, Steven DeKosky, Sr. Mercy deLeon, Mark Dettmann, Dawn Dole, Lise Uyanik Ebel, Marta Erhard, Suzanne Fey-Gaiser, Claire Fialkov, Bruce Flye, Dorrie Fontaine, Sharon Franquemont, Ron Fry

Patricia Gallivan, Mary and Ken Gergen, Charles Gibbs, Sr. Mary Ann Giordano, Sr. Jude Ellen Golumbieski, Mike Goodu, Amy Gorely, Jim Grady, Rita Guild

David Haddad, Julie Haizlip, Barbara Hartford, Rebecca Heckman, Allan Henderson, Carol Henderson, Margaret Henderson, Peggy Holman, Ed Howell

Jeff Jackson and Maurice Monette, Dennis Jaffe, Gil Judson, Tom Kaney, Judy Keene, Paul Kelly, Ashwani Khurana, Nancy Kriplen

Peter Lang, Sr. Brigid Lawlor, Stewart Levine, Barbara Lewis, Jessica and Don Lewis, Martin Little, Jim Lord, Jim Ludema

Natalie Mae, Sally Mahe, Debbie Mangum, Julie Manhard, Mike Mantel, Suzanne and John Mariner, Laurie Maslak, Sr. Mary Catherine Massei, Elspeth McAdam, Carol McLaurin, Sheila McNamee, Kurt Meletzke, Carolyn Miller, Bernard Mohr, Amshatar Monroe, Peter Morales, Carlos Aguilera Muga, Sr. Madeleine Munday

Takafumi Nawa, Gary Nelson, Deb Nickell, Dick Notebaert, Kelle Olwyler, Rick Pellett, Marge Perry, Peggy Plews-Ogan, Tenny Poole, Bob Possanza, Phillipe Poulin

Sonja Radatz, Anne Radford, Nila Reinhart, Rosemary Richardson, John Rijsman, Dana and Jim Robinson, Myron Rogers, Frank Rogers-Witte, Karen Roney, Jim and Sue Rose

Marge Schiller, Judith Schuster, JwaSeop Shin, John Shorling, John Shotter, Patti Smith, Nancy Southern, Betsy Stang, Jackie Stavros, Julie Stockton, Suresh Srivastva, Bill Swing, Sr. Clare Szlachetka

Emiko Takama, Kunio Takama, Johanna Vodeling, Jane Watkins and Ralph Kelly, Ralph Weickel, Greg Welch, Anne Williams, Rosemary Williams, Tish Wilson, Susan Wood, Danielle Zande, Andrea Zintz

Artemis, Calgary Health Region, Colorado Springs Leadership Institute, El Pomar Foundation, Green Mountain Coffee Roasters, Hewlett-Packard, Human Value, Japan, Hunter Douglas WFD, Leadership Pikes Peak, Sanchez-Tennis and Associates, Sisters of the Good Shepherd PMNA, The Mentoring Company, The Taos Institute, The Vallarta Institute, United Religions Initiative, U.S. Anti-Doping Agency, University of Virginia Health System

INDEX

About the Authors

Diana Whitney, Ph.D., President of Corporation for Positive Change is an inspirational keynote speaker, executive advisor, and visionary thought leader on Appreciative Leadership and Positive Change. She is a master consultant using Appreciative Inquiry—the revolutionary process she helped to develop and introduce in over 30 countries—for large scale transformation and strategic culture change in business, healthcare, education, and religious organizations. Her award winning writing has positively influenced the lives of millions of people around the world. She has authored or edited fifteen books, dozens of articles and chapters, and designed the Appreciative Leadership Development Program©, now available through an international network of certified trainers. She is a founder of the Taos Institute, a Distinguished Consulting Faculty with Saybrook University, and a fellow of the World Business Academy. She can be reached at Diana@positivechange.org.

Amanda Trosten-Bloom, Managing Director of Corporation for Positive Change, is a widely acclaimed consultant, master trainer, and energizing speaker. She is a pioneer in the use of Appreciative Inquiry for high engagement, whole system change in business, nonprofit, and community settings. Amanda builds results-oriented partnerships with executives and their teams in support of strategic planning, culture change, and organizational excellence. Her award-winning work in high-tech, service, manufacturing, and municipal sectors has been prominently featured in dozens of books and articles. She is the author of four books, including *The Power of Appreciative Inquiry* and *The Encyclopedia of Positive Questions*. She can be reached at Amanda@positivechange.org.

Kae Rader, President of Rader Consulting and Consulting Partner with Corporation for Positive Change, is a results-oriented consultant, dynamic facilitator, and speaker. She works with leadership teams to build collaborative, high-performing cultures, formulate strategy, and develop operating plans to drive and reward performance. She also advises nonprofit clients on governance best practices. Kae has held senior management positions with the U.S. Olympic Committee, Indiana Sports Corporation, and El Pomar Foundation. She holds a Master's in Public Administration and a Graduate Certificate in Nonprofit Management from the University of Colorado. She can be reached at Kae@positivechange.org.